Gisela Hagemann

# The motivation manual

Gower

© Gisela Hagemann 1992

First published in hardback 1992
Reprinted 1993

This paperback edition published by
Gower Publishing
Gower House
Croft Road
Aldershot
Hants GU11 3HR
England

Gower
Old Post Road
Brookfield
Vermont 05036
USA

A CIP catalogue record for this book is available from the British
Library.

ISBN 0–566–07295–5 (Hbk)
      0–566–07618–7 (Pbk)

Typeset in 11 point Times by Photoprint, Torquay, Devon
Printed in England by Hartnolls Ltd, Bodmin

# Acknowledgement

I should like to thank Lynda Lich-Knight for her help in preparing the English-language version of this book, which she translated from the German edition.

GH

# Contents

**Appendices**

# Introduction

You can force someone to do something, but you can never actually force him to want to do it. The desire to want comes from within us, and motivation is the internal driving force which elicits pleasure from work: feeling good and efficiency are very closely related.

Whether a company is able to meet the challenges of the nineties depends on its ability to mobilize human potential. Good leadership assures an advantage over your competitors.

The most important source of innovation within a company is the individual employee. High producitivity is determined not only by modern technology, but also by people's attitudes: are we prepared to commit ourselves? Do we identify with the objectives of the company, and are we willing to dedicate ourselves to achieving them? Or do we find ourselves constantly looking at the clock, bored stiff, and groaning: 'Roll on five o'clock'?

The quality of human relationships influences economic results decisively. When the manager and the rest of the staff are on the same wavelength they can create the ideal situation for turning the survival strategies of the eighties into the success strategies of the nineties. When talk of openness, trust and mutual respect is not just hot air, the daily routine loses much of its banality.

An assertive manager knows that the authority arising from his personality, and above all from his ability to deal with people, is far superior to the formal power vested in position and status. A manager who believes he can only maintain the dignity of his position by keeping his subordinates at a distance merely does harm to himself. It is, however, just as erroneous to attempt to win

ix

people over by letting them do whatever they want. Too little leadership is just as frustrating as too much.

A happy medium can be achieved by creating a shared vision, ensuring the free flow of information and allowing the staff to participate in the decision-making process.

When people with different interests, experience and conceptions of reality come together, friction is inevitable. Conflicts simmering just below the surface eventually boil over, and the employees become totally immersed in their own thoughts. Someone who feels unjustly treated becomes resigned and vindictive. Work takes a back seat. However, if the leadership manages to harness this released energy creatively and constructively, such conflicts can turn into a power-house for dynamic development.

Naturally, all of this assumes that the boss and the staff do talk to each other, not least about unpleasant things. If the managers keep themselves to themselves on the top floor, while below them the rest of the staff are busy airing their grievances on the grapevine, they deprive themselves of the opportunity of reaching a better mutual understanding. If they can get to know each other as people, and communicate their hopes and fears, they will be better able to find solutions which are acceptable to everyone.

Working in a team means constantly solving problems, and the form which cooperation takes is thus decisive. People are motivated by creative, participatory working methods, and this reduces the ever-present potential for conflict, especially as in the final analysis a considerable number of protests are really only a desperate cry for attention. If, by contrast, people have the feeling of belonging and being listened to, they start to identify with the objectives of the company. Even more deep-seated conflicts of interest are easier to settle if the opposing factions lay their cards on the table.

Working methods need to be efficient and structured in such a way that conclusions really can be reached in an acceptable period of time. A meeting at which the boss holds forth at length while the others sit silently nodding their heads is a waste of time for all concerned. In such cases, written directives would be more effective and more honest. If, on the other hand, everyone insists on having his say, and people find themselves attending eternally long, unstructured and badly prepared meetings, staff participation turns into a farce. No progress can be made because there is always someone who just has to pop off and fetch some supplementary information, someone else who wants to revoke an earlier decision, and yet a third person who wishes to postpone a new one.

This book is a collection of ideas on modern management which also contains practical assistance in the form of examples and exercises. As a management consultant I am only too aware that it is not enough to ask "what?" but, above all, "how?".

It is my wish to contribute to strengthening cooperation within companies, and so I have written this book for all those who prefer to convince others of their point of view, rather than ordering them around and then feeling depressed because nobody listens to them. It is our own behaviour which causes people to react in ways we often find so difficult to accept. Every one of us is responsible for the consequences of our actions.

This book invites both managers and staff to communicate with each other in order to break down the mental barrier which assumes that the manager has an exclusive right to visions while the rest of the staff are reduced to the passive role of carrying out orders.

A company's internal resources can be utilized more advantageously. One of the reasons why the millions spent on managerial development have only produced a few lasting results is that management by objectives, organizational development and personal mastery have been taking place in isolation (see Figure 1). Traditionally, top management considered themselves responsible for goals and strategy, and left organizational development to external consultants and internal steering committees, with the minimum of personal involvement on their own part. When times were good, companies decided to send their staff on courses; when times were bad, the in-service training budget was the first to fall victim to cut-backs.

In the past few years, organizational development has usually

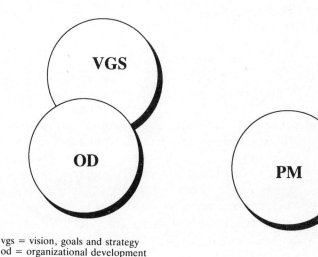

vgs = vision, goals and strategy
od = organizational development
pm = personal mastery

*Figure 1*

been understood to mean cutting costs. As undertakings of this kind are seldom popular, many managers choose the supposedly easier path of excluding their staff from the internal process of change. When all decisions are concentrated at the top, without those affected having an opportunity to influence their own working situation, managers are unable to mobilize their staff's creativity. Many will only bow to orders from above grudgingly, and with obvious frustration. There will be a good deal of whispering in the corridors, and efficiency will suffer. As a consequence, things become worse than is necessary. It is, therefore, definitely worthwhile involving staff in the work of reorganization.

A successful company makes sure that it is not only the managers, but also the staff who can find a ready ear for their suggestions. Obviously, it is impossible for all new ideas to be adopted, but this is certainly no excuse for consigning them to the waste-paper basket. All suggestions, whether good or bad, have the right to be aired, and the modern manager prides himself on being able to explain why an idea is untenable. Time taken to clarify objectives or substantiate an argument is not wasted. Indeed, if word gets round in the company that new ideas are taken seriously, the collective ability to think along new lines will grow accordingly, and this is the only way in which the entire potential of an organization can be utilized. And this, in its turn, presupposes free and open communication.

In order to develop an organization we have to develop individual people. This book thus combines shared vision, organizational development and personal mastery to create a unity (as shown in Figure 2).

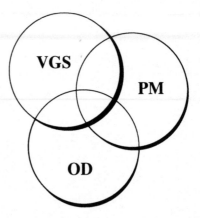

vgs = vision, goals and strategy
od = organizational development
pm = personal mastery

*Figure 2*

Further evidence in support of my ideas can be found in Peter M. Senge's book *The Fifth Discipline*, where he notes, for example, 'Organizations learn only through individuals who learn. Individual learning does not guarantee organizational learning. But without it no organizational learning occurs . . . Kazuori Inamori . . . says this: Whether it is research and development, company management, or any other aspect of business, the active force is people. And people have their own will, their own mind, and their own way of thinking. If the employees themselves are not sufficiently motivated to challenge the goals of growth and technological development . . . there will simply be no growth, no gain in productivity and no technological development.'

In times of such dramatic change as the present, the following target groups in particular should find this book useful: managers who are planning the reorganization of a company, or who are already in the middle of a restructuring process; consultants in the field of leadership training and personal development; personnel managers; those responsible for company-based in-service training; teachers and students of management science; indeed, anyone who has to deal with people on a regular basis and whose task it is to be convincing, whether as a salesperson, the leader of a project-group, or the chairperson of a meeting.

# Part I—Motivation and organizational change

# 1 | Creating a shared vision

A vision of the future and the motivation to put it into action have always been important; they have now become a matter of survival. Times have changed, and we can no longer sit around quietly waiting to see how things will turn out, or mull over decisions at our leisure.

We can either use up all our energy trying to avoid change, or we can choose to recognize opportunities rather than barriers. In this context it is worth bearing 'The New Leaders' Mission Statement in mind: 'The more we understand the nature of change we are facing, the easier it is to accept its inevitability, and prepare to benefit from it. The less we understand it, the greater is the tendency to fight it, to resist it as if our very lives depended upon maintaining the status quo.'

## The balance between hard and soft values

The challenge a company faces is to complete the difficult process of transformation by achieving a balance between clear objectives ('hard values') on the one hand, and stimulating a positive culture ('soft values') on the other. Visions show the way forward, but in order to put them into action a manager is dependent on mobilizing his staff's creativity and dedication. Corporate culture is the way we do things; it can be the difference between pouring either oil or sand into a machine. A positive culture enables visions to become a reality. This is the most important means of achieving objectives.

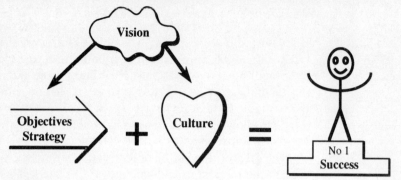

**A shared vision + clear objectives + positive culture = success**

*Figure 3*

| **Objective and strategy** | **Corporate culture** |
|---|---|
| What? | How? |
| Task orientated | People orientated |
| ('Hard values') | ('Soft values') |
| | |
| *Effectiveness* | *Identification with goal* |
| technology | participation, enthusiasm |
| economic control | self-realization, recognition |
| | |
| *Knowledge and competence* | *Motivation* |
| expertise in the field | willingness to learn something new |
| recruiting and retaining | good working atmosphere, |
| qualified people | challenges participation |
| | |
| *Quality* | *Communication and cooperation* |
| technical success | internally: mutual trust |
| on-time | free flow of |
| on-budget | information |
| | open communication, |
| project control | constructive feedback |
| | externally: good service |
| | interest in client's |
| | requirements |

What demands are made on managers by the challenges of the future? How do factors such as a shared vision, clear goals, and a positive corporate culture influence prospects for success? All of these factors require us to be optimistic and realistic, caring and demanding, creative and practical at one and the same time.

# A positive attitude to change

4 In the past, companies could respond to clients' demands. Now

companies have to act before their clients have appreciated their own problems.

One of the preconditions for flexibility is that employees are empowered to make decisions within their own fields of responsibility. Of course, in pursuing new paths you are always in danger of stumbling into obstacles. If a minor mistake automatically means that future career prospects are at an end, no-one will have the courage to take any risks at all. Thus every single employee must be allowed to ask questions, make mistakes, and point out necessary improvements before it is too late.

The greater the degree of motivation within the workforce, the greater the interest in and willingness to react to signals indicating what is going on in and around the company. Free and open communication is the only way to ensure that information reaches those responsible in good time. And this shows to what a great extent the success of changes in strategy on the macro-level is governed by what happens on the micro-level within a company.

In future, a state of constant flux will have to be accepted as the norm. Many companies have already realized that there is no point in making complex long-term prognoses – anything might intervene. While in the past companies drew up plans for a period of ten years, they now confine themselves to between three and five. In future, managers will frequently find themselves in the position of having to make decisions on the basis of zero-data. This requires intuition and a delicate nose for those social, political and technological innovations which, sooner or later, might be of consequence for the company.

Everyone has to learn how to make decisions in the face of uncertainty, and how to retain a positive attitude even during periods of turbulent change. Characteristics such as empathy, intuition, the ability to adjust, and not least of all a sound knowledge of human nature, are essential to this process. The 'old-fashioned' values of mutual respect, reliability and altruism emerge as essential ingredients to success.

If there is to be any hope of achieving a reorganization it is not enough simply to alter formal structures by drawing new boxes and squares on the organizational plan and joining them together with little lines. What is far more significant is what is happening within the individual units. What is the working atmosphere like? Are the staff part of an active team, or are they only passive observers watching the game from a distance?

Organizational development often begins with a diagnosis of the present state, and in some cases this can, indeed, be the right point of departure. However, there is always the danger that organizations spend so much time raking over the ground that the analysis turns into an all-out search for a scapegoat. Without the

5

guidance of a competent external consultant the working environment may well become worse than it was before.

A much more positive starting point is when managers and staff pool their visions for the future. One of the most important motivating factors is the feeling of belonging to a group. Exceptional power can be discovered in the community which identifies with a vision.

## Making the vision real

A vision is a mental journey from the known to the unknown. What will the company be like in five years time? What can be achieved if we use a bit of imagination, and put all restrictions to one side for the time being? Who or what is preventing us from making our dreams come true? How can we overcome these obstacles? How can we build up trust in ourselves and in each other?

Visioning differs from traditional management by objectives because it is not restricted to the intellectual investigation of possibilities, but also stimulates mental images, fantasy and intuition, encouraging us to clarify our objectives and strengthen our belief in our ability to achieve them. All of us have a great deal more potential than we make use of under normal circumstances. The point is to release the hidden resources in order to create a unity of brain and heart. In this way we are not merely trying to predict the future, but to take an active part in forming it. This gives us the feeling of controlling our own lives. We are not just putty in someone else's hands. We ourselves are responsible for creating the sort of reality we want. Creative visualization is a supplementary method to management by objectives, and a practical tool for dealing with everyday reality (cf. exercise 16).

If a vision is going to become real we have to work on it together. Participation is important for achieving identification. Every day we make small and large choices. Only when our internal values and our external behaviour are in unison will we intuitively do what will lead us to our objective. Thus a consensus about our purpose (cf. exercise 15) is a precondition for maintaining our courage even during difficult times.

A welcome side-effect of visioning is coping with stress. We are most creative in a so-called Alpha-state. This is a transition phase between sleeping and waking which each of us experiences at least twice a day. With the help of relaxation exercises we can consciously achieve this state. When we are relaxed it is easier to think positively.

# Clearly defined objectives

You must know what you want. Your energy, knowledge and perseverance must be directed towards a goal, and this goal must be clear, concrete and specific. It should be realistic while being optimistic. On top of this, you have to do something in order to reach your goal.

A vision is a kind of overriding objective which we can compare with a light illuminating a path in the darkness. When you manage to make your objective concrete and describe it precisely in terms of a desired outcome, the light becomes concentrated into a laser beam, so strong that it can cut through a wall. Only when you can see your objective quite clearly in front of you, and identify yourself with it whole-heartedly, will you be able to make the right decisions, spontaneously.

Try to penetrate to the heart of the matter. What is it you want in essence? If you get rid of the inessentials, what is left over? What is the supreme issue? What is really important to you? What do you need in order to reach your goal? We frequently find ourselves fighting for one thing when we are actually after something completely different.

The following examples illustrate the point:

A young woman wants to go to Africa to work in development aid. When asking herself the above questions she discovers that what she really wants is more human contact. She thought that she had to do something particular ('help the poor') in order to 'deserve' other people's gratitude and attention. The challenge she faces is to work on her relations with people here and now before attempting to go off to save others. Amongst other things, this requires her to risk taking the initiative herself, and overcome her fear of being rejected.

A female lawyer requests a red light over the door of her office to indicate when she is engaged. When asking herself the question as to what lies at the very heart of her requirement, she discovers that what she is really after is to be respected by and considered equal to her male colleagues, who all have red lights over their doors. The need for a good working atmosphere and recognition can be satisfied in other ways, without resorting to red lights.

Concomitantly, there are many people who want more money to ensure greater security. If we are not in harmony with ourselves emotionally, all the riches in the world will not give us peace of mind. You can find examples of senile millionaires who literally drown in their own dirt because they refuse to employ professional help for fear of being robbed.

By investing a little thought in describing your desired outcome as concretely as possible, you will encounter possibilities which you would not otherwise have thought of. You do not need to wait until the children have grown up, the mortgage is paid off, or the premium bonds have come up in order to be happy. By concentrating on the very essence of what you want to achieve you will become more flexible. There are always a number of paths leading to the same goal.

You have to know what you want to say, express yourself clearly, and get your ideas accepted. Exercise 1 is a checklist designed to help you to bring clarity into a discussion or written communication. Exercise 3 shows you how to sell your ideas. Exercise 5 assists you with stating clear-cut demands.

In her book *Influencing with Integrity*, Genie Z. Laborde compares communication to a journey. First you make a decision about where you want to go. Then you think about how you are going to get there, and whom you want to invite to go with you. If you want to travel from London to Edinburgh you can go by plane, by car or by rail. If you decide to drive you have to choose the best route. You need road signs en route telling you whether you are still travelling in the right direction. If your passengers are heading for a different destination they have to find out where they have to get out in order to continue their journey alone. When you finally reach Edinburgh you have to find out whether this is really the place you want to visit. Is it really here where you can get what you want?

Just as a journey begins with determining the destination, a process of communication begins with discovering what results you want to achieve. To communicate without having your objective clearly in mind is like getting on a train without checking where it is going.

## Positive objectives

Focus on what you want, and not on what you do not want. A positive message is more motivating than a negative one. You are 'in favour of mutual trust and respect', not 'against group aggression'. You are 'in favour of a good working environment', not 'against bad management'.

There is a limit to the amount of negative information the individual can take in. Think about yourself: from the moment you get up in the morning and turn on the radio until you watch the late news at night you are confronted with wars, crises and catastrophes, earthquakes, violence, accidents, corruption, environmental scandals, economic problems and personal tragedies. Many people cannot cope with more than this. They feel apathetic and powerless.

If you want to bring about change you have to show that it is useful, and that every single person has the opportunity to contribute something positive. If you merely criticize the state of things you create a negative atmosphere.

You are constantly transmitting signals with your body language. Your thoughts are mirrored in your facial expression, your posture and your voice. Do you have a glint in your eye and a smile on your lips, or are you clenching your teeth in frustration? Is your posture relaxed, or are you straining your neck muscles and wishing you were invisible? It is impossible not to communicate. Irrespective of what you say or do you are transmitting signals, and these either attract or repel other people.

Your negative thoughts make you appear negative. What you achieve by speaking disparagingly of others may be that your competitor gets a bad reputation, but it will not mean that people start looking up to you. People will not rely on a person who stabs others in the back. The people you are with will be on their guard: 'If he talks about others behind their backs he probably also gossips about me!' Thus talk rather about the advantages of your own suggestions than of the disadvantages of others' ideas.

Do not waste your energies being jealous of other people's success. If you hate a person he has control over you. You need time and energy to think about him – time which you could rather use to do something productive. You cannot free yourself of something until you have made peace with yourself inside. You are emotionally bound up with people you dislike. Only by forgiving them will you be able to free yourself.

Do not wait for others to do things for you before getting enthusiastic. You yourself must ensure that the work you do is not a weighty burden, but an opportunity to realize yourself. Things you are pleased to do for others will provide you yourself with personal satisfaction. Rely rather on convincing others than on criticizing them. Talk about opportunities instead of problems.

## Strategy

When your goal is clear you can start preparing a strategy (cf. exercises 18–20). The best strategy is of no use whatsoever if the company is not in a position to put it into practice.

Organizations are made up of individual people. They are human beings and not an anonymous apparatus for producing results. It is, therefore, important that each individual recognizes his own significance in achieving the common objective. In order to realize a strategy, i.e. to carry out what we have decided upon, we need to have a corporate culture which motivates staff to pull their weight. Motivation can be encouraged by satisfying people's need to feel they belong, are appreciated, and can realize themselves. The corporate culture (*how*) is thus just as important as the plan of action (*what*).

## Focus and flexibility

In order to reach your goal your actions must be focused on that goal. You create what you want by forming a picture of it in your mind, and concentrate your full attention on it. Always have it at the back of your mind, even when you are doing other things. This will ensure that you are alert and grasp opportunities as they present themselves.

In the absence of clear priorities you are constantly in danger of trying to do too many things at once, ending up totally burnt out without having got anywhere. You are not a world champion who can do everything equally well; apart from which, there are only 24 hours in any one day. Concentrate your energies and resources on completing your tasks one after the other. Even if it is sometimes tempting and flattering to say yes every time you are asked, you are in danger of becoming so diversified that you end up doing everything superficially. It may then happen that you do not have enough time to read the documents referring to an important meeting. The consequences of this are that you do not achieve your goal, and do a poor job. Bear in mind that there are others who would welcome the chance of a challenge. Exercise 17 is a step-by-step reminder on how to keep your focus while staying flexible.

## Willpower

In order to achieve your objective you have to show willpower and perseverance. You have to believe in your objective and the path you have chosen to achieve it. You have to love doing what is required of you. Your will to strive onward focuses your energies on your goal.

When there is a huge gulf between objective and reality we tend to get impatient. The whole world seems to be conspiring against us. Everyone else just breezes along; we are the only ones who have to plod on. It is so unjust! The gap between the current situation and the desired result is called *creative tension*. Instead of feeling sorry for yourself, try to see it as a source of energy driving you on to tackle something which will bring you closer to your objective.

Keep believing in yourself when you experience the odd setback. Do not let defeat mean defeat, but take it as a chance to learn: What went wrong? Why did it go wrong? What can I do better next time? The difference between success and defeat is perseverance.

Obstacles and resistance help you to grow strong, and to rely on your own resources. By overcoming obstacles you build up your self-confidence. What looks like an insurmountable barrier might actually open up new and better ways. The challenge is to find out whether the resistance you encounter means that you should rethink your strategy, or whether opposition will help you to build up strength which will lead to your goal.

# 2 | Motivation and change

Demographic trends reveal a growth in the number of older people, while the percentage of younger people is declining. Improbable as it may seem in view of high unemployment, in a few years time the economy will start to suffer from falling numbers among the well-qualified workforce. Access to potential employees with sound training and relevant experience could become the main factor affecting future growth. Young people with good qualifications will be able to pick and choose their jobs, and even the prospect of substantial salaries will not suffice in the fight to attract competent staff and gain their loyalty. Another competitor is sure to be able to offer more. For many people a stimulating working atmosphere, active participation and opportunities for personal development are much more important than money. One of the greatest challenges to the company is to realize that managers have to learn to become really good at man-management.

## People-orientated management

Not enough managers think about their own role. They have achieved their current high position due to their earlier success in their specialized field, but instead of becoming a true authority, showing others the way forward, they tend to turn themselves into glorified reps and assistants. To be certain that capable experts do not end up as inadequate bosses, a great deal more attention should be given to the personal characteristics of applicants seeking managerial positions.

The ability to motivate and to work in a team is just as important as know-how and an analytical mind. The lone-wolf at the top cannot manage everything alone any more. The problems are getting more complex, and call for unorthodox solutions and interdisciplinary cooperation. For this reason, future managers will be much more dependent on the knowledge and loyalty of their staff; thus they are clearly acting in their own interests when they show their staff just as much attention and respect as they show their best customers.

The leadership-style adopted by the boss determines the amount of effort made by the staff. Despite the huge cultural differences between Europe and Japan, and the fact that not everything which happens there would be possible or even desirable here, in the field of motivation Japan is exemplary. In an interview for the West German magazine *Der Spiegel*, the boss of Sony, Akio Morita, whose company has a worldwide turnover of roughly DM30 billion, reveals the secret of his success, 'Communication, genuine communication – that's the most important thing.' Elsewhere he notes 'The essential point is to give people something to aim for.' He continues, 'It's all about creativity. For many years I have been in charge of a creative company and I know how to motivate creative people. I would never tell them what to do and what not to do.'

In an interview with *Stern* magazine, the American head of Sony in Germany, Ron Sommer, reports 'Every single employee has to identify with Sony and Sony's products, otherwise it just wouldn't work. I'm more likely to get into trouble with Japan if motivation and the working atmosphere are in a poor state than I am if the figures are not so good.'

In the same way that the Japanese think long-term when they invest in research and development, they know that investing in people and the working environment make economic sense.

A manager who wants to achieve excellent results ignores the psychological well-being of his staff at his peril. This is especially important as the balance of power within companies is in the process of shifting in favour of employees with higher qualifications.

The skilled staff of an electronics company can make higher demands on the leadership-style and the working atmosphere, as they are in a position of far greater power than their unskilled colleagues who can easily be replaced by other workers.

Consider the differences between a miner/steel worker and a computer specialist/highly-qualified engineer. Working in the mines is merely a way of earning a living, with no relation whatsoever to concepts like self-realization. The miner fights for higher wages, a shorter working-week, and better accident prevention. Hard physical labour eventually undermines both physical and mental energy, and the miner welcomes retirement with open arms.

By contrast, the staff of a high-tech company tend to do too little rather than too much physical work, but with a healthy diet and plenty of sport they can sustain their creative and productive energies well into old age. Their knowledge gives them power: they cannot easily be replaced by others, and their practical experience is of considerable value to the company. Strikes frequently reveal that quite small groups can force whole areas of life to break down completely. If, on top of this, the number of specialists available drops, their existing position of strength is made even stronger.

Managers with vision look for contact with people. Just by talking to the staff a manager can feel in his own body the vibrations at ground level. By shutting themselves in their own rooms and burying their heads in paperwork, managers miss out on such close contact.

In order to mobilize the staff it is necessary to be orientated towards people. Psychological research reveals that 95% of our decisions are made on the emotional level – however well we may parcel up our motives in apparently rational reasoning. We feel hurt and passed over, and say we have not had the time to do a certain job. We feel unjustly treated, and say we have had a professional disagreement.

## Lifelong learning

Knowledge is power. If you want to be one of those forging the future rather than feeling yourself to be a victim of circumstances, you have to keep up. It is no longer legitimate for a woman to say 'I can't read this book/these documents because I am married with two kids', or for a man to claim 'Now the shooting season is opening. Work can wait.' You must keep your knowledge up to date, and you are never too old to learn something new.

As the numbers of graduates from colleges and universities will soon be too low to cater for the needs of industry, companies are well advised to start ensuring their resources now by nurturing their contacts with colleges and universities, and by turning their attention to in-service training.

To prevent employees from stagnating by simply continuing to do what they have always done, they need new ideas. Opportunities for professional development and personal mastery are thus neither charity, a gift, nor a luxury for the financially successful years, but an investment in the future.

The aim of personnel development is to encourage people to take responsibility. To make independent decisions within the spheres delegated to them, staff need to be informed well in advance of what is supposed to happen, and why. Each individual must be sure that he can express his opinions without fear of reprisals.

Motivation is a product of participation, but working together is not easy. Nonetheless, the rules of inter-human relations can be learned, and for this reason it is not sufficient just to pursue professional development; it is equally important to encourage social competence.

Continuity is central to achieving lasting results. Short, open seminars can throw up important new ideas, but they do not alter entrenched patterns of behaviour. Experience shows that internal measures, including both individual coaching and group follow-up, lead to the best results.

If training in communication and cooperation is really going to be taken seriously, managers and staff should participate in the same measures. As long as managers go on exclusive management courses while staff have to be satisfied with separate development courses on the cheap, the danger is that people will only learn with their heads and not with their hearts, i.e. that the manager will get the message on an intellectual level, but will not be able to change his behaviour in practice. The real challenge is for everyone concerned to deal with both negative and positive relations in the workplace face-to-face.

The time has come to undertake a re-appraisal of current training methods. The way in which a topic is presented determines whether, and how quickly, the message will be understood and subsequently put into practice. Long monologue-lectures seldom inspire independent thinking. Conversely, consultants who confuse in-service training with 'show business', and feel it incumbent upon themselves to 'entertain' their audience, do not achieve lasting results either.

Adults want to take an active part in the process, making use of their abilities. In future, developing creative training and working-methods with which people can identify could become an attractive growth market.

A pleasant, relaxed atmosphere is conducive to reaching in-service training goals more quickly. A session during which people become aware of their own style of communication, and the use of unconscious signals transmitted by body language and voice, should be an integral part of every developmental seminar. Deep breathing and relaxation raise the level of concentration, and counteract stress. In Japan, quality circles frequently begin with everyone doing breathing exercises in unison. I have found it very advantageous to begin and end every day of a course or project meeting with relaxation and creative visualization (cf. exercise 16).

It has now been scientifically proven that the body and soul form a unity. American researchers have managed to show that a direct exchange of information takes place between the nerves and the cells responsible for the body's immune system. The state of our emotions influences the state of our health. A person who is tuned in to their emotions and is prepared to reveal them is not only helping himself to remain healthy, but is also contributing to his level of achievement.

Many managers have realized that movement helps to prevent illness, and they now encourage employees to keep fit at the company's expense. It could be just as important to begin each working day with half an hour of relaxation and creative visualization of the company's objectives, including a short round of 'How are you today?' A couple of minutes per person is sufficient. The point is that every member of staff gets the chance to mention anything he is concerned about. Once a week it is necessary to have a more thorough discussion about what has been happening.

I am also in favour of offering staff facilities for massage during working hours, especially as one hour spent in this way per week is more than compensated for by reduced stress and illness, fewer conflicts, and greater effort. Top managers in the United States have long since grasped the connection between physical and psychological well-being, and they consequently make an appointment with their masseur part of their daily routine.

The old adage about learning for life can take on a totally new meaning. Many older people feel that their lives are enriched by learning something new at an advanced age; some even embark on a second or third course of study.

The former vice-president of the International Association of Accelerative Learning, the American Dee Dickinson, has suggested that state schools should remain open in the afternoons, evenings and during the holidays so that not only employers, managers and students, but also ordinary employees, can start to prepare for the difficult tasks awaiting us in the future. She cites the small town of Anacortes on the west coast of Washington State as a shining example of what can be done. There they have been putting these ideas into practice by organizing an active school-exchange programme with Japan. Americans are now learning Japanese, and this has led to a considerable growth in trade with Japan (source: *Management Wissen*).

Hierarchical structures do not nurture creativity and thus, in future, companies will require more flexible organizational structuring.

**16**

# From hierarchies to networks

Hierarchical structures tend to be cumbersome. Usually, communication within such companies only flows in one direction: from the boss down to the subordinates, and even if the latter do come up with ideas and suggestions, they are seldom taken seriously. Authoritarian managers immediately assume they are being criticized personally, and nip such behaviour in the bud, just to be on the safe side. In some cases, it is so difficult to force suggested changes through the vagaries of the system, that they never penetrate at all, or if they do only in a watered-down version.

I was called in by a subsidiary of a large company, where processing times were getting ever longer and profits sinking accordingly, to restructure the organization and working routines. The project began with an organizational diagnosis seminar for both the management and staff. The aim was to collate everyone's suggestions for improvement in a brain-storming session. This was the first opportunity the staff had ever had to voice their opinions, and they made full use of it. The manager was immensely shocked. Normally he had little contact with his staff, and thus suffered from the illusion that they were all one big happy family. Instead of taking the time to give thought to suggestions from the staff, he came back the next day and rejected them out of hand. He fought bitterly against every attempt to introduce more effective working routines, or a more efficient distribution of duties. Any change would have meant conceding that something was not right somewhere.

The staff, who had been very keen at the beginning, soon lost interest in the project. They noticed that the boss got angry when they did not agree with him, and treated them like troublemakers when they dared to say what they thought. They soon reverted to their old apathy, and one person summed up the situation in the following words: 'I'm scared of opening my mouth. After all, I have to turn up for work again tomorrow.'

The attitude of the manager is reflected in the staff of a company. If the manager wants to achieve something he has to set a good example; he will only be credible if he practises what he preaches.

A company which aims to be adaptable has to say farewell to the concept of a hierarchy. Future organizational forms will consist partly of fixed structures and partly of flexible forms of cooperation. Those tasks which constantly recur in exactly the same form can continue to be organized according to a fixed pattern, while creative tasks or those which vary in the course of time, can be assigned to project groups or informal networks. For this to work, free and open communication is necessary so that everybody knows exactly what he or she is supposed to be doing. Companies which distribute large projects among various sub-groups enable their staff to gain practical experience and carry out on-the-job-training. New and progressively difficult tasks build up competence. Changes no longer come as a shock, but are an integral feature of the average working day.

To prevent the empire from splitting up into a host of petty principalities, it is essential to bind all the strands together at the top. This can be done by arranging regular consultations between the top manager and the project group leaders, at which improvements in purchasing, technology and productivity can be discussed and brought to a conclusion.

Working together in self-regulating groups has proven to be very good for motivation, but it does make high demands on the team-spirit and self-discipline of all concerned. What is good for one's own group is not necessarily in the best interests of the company as a whole. A project-group leader may be tempted to retain a particularly capable colleague for his own purposes, even if he does not really have much use for him at present, while another group is crying out for someone. By prioritizing his own advantage, an 'egoistic' project-leader will increase his profit and improve his career prospects while the company suffers because another group has not been given the help it required.

Conflicts of this kind between individual achievement and overall result also exist in companies which work a bonus-system, as colleagues can end up vying for each other's clients. It is therefore extremely important that recognition and reward are not only accorded in relation to individual economic results, but also to the will and ability to work together for the good of the whole.

Cooperation at the workplace is more effective than internal competition. The best way of achieving your own objective is to make sure that your colleagues also achieve theirs. Always try to find a solution which makes both sides feel that they have won.

If you do experience conflicts with others, reconsider your own attitude: do not automatically assume that it is the other person who is holding something against you. Make it a rule that your opponent should be able to save face. You will be serving your own interests best if you maintain a good working relationship with everybody.

The best way of ensuring good cooperation is to collate people's expectations in advance, and arrive at a common conception of reality (cf. exercises 12, 13, 22 and 26). By anticipating what might occur at a later stage we can avoid conflicts and misunderstandings.

In the case of project groups covering various fields, the rules determining internal team cooperation and the relationship to the environment should be considered in advance. Exercise 24 shows you how to proceed so as to make people function together as a superteam.

## Interaction all round

Price and quality are two important factors influencing the customer's decision to buy. In future, however, this decision will also be governed by the joint effects of various factors.

A firm which produces accident life-saving equipment can be of assistance in an advisory capacity in training medical personnel, and in servicing the equipment. In the field of computers the trend is towards integrated, ready-made product solutions comprising hardware, software, supply and support training. As the mix of products gets more complicated, the suppliers require not only a better knowledge of the field, but also a more comprehensive customer service. All the knowledge in the world on computers is of no use whatsoever if the attitude to service is inferior, or if an expert is unable to make himself understood by his customers.

A conference hotel gets a bad name if the telephone switchboard is constantly engaged, and when callers do finally get through they are told 'I'm afraid the lady in charge of bookings is not available at present'.
'What would be the best time to ring back?'
'I don't know. It's pretty hectic around here all day.'

A company which is unable to accept an order is not very confidence-inspiring. Why is there no-one at reservations? Why is there no-one to take a message? Why is there no-one to ring clients back? Similarly, a hotel gets a bad name when it sends six invoices for five courses and, even after the mistake has been cleared up by 'phone, has the audacity to send reminders for payment. If the telephone switchboard and the conference and accounts departments are not coordinated, then it is of little comfort that the rooms are nice and the food is good.

## Women: the neglected resource

To make people enthusiastic we need a corporate culture focusing on cooperation and identification, instead of on power struggles and intrigue.

The most modern demands on future managers have a great deal in common with those traditional values which women start learning the moment they are born. Even little girls are aware that they should care for others. Later, in taking responsibility for a family, they become experienced in team-work, administration and budgeting. The challenge which women face, however, is how to apply the social competence gained in the home to the wider field of society as a whole. A step of this kind requires self-confidence, and also the opportunity to gather experience at progressively difficult job levels. By adopting a specific policy of encouraging women, companies can gain even greater assets than they originally realize.

As children get older, most women would like to return to work. Many of them have valuable working experience from before, and can bring their knowledge up to date. Such women are often extremely enthusiastic and full of initiatives because they are pleased to be able to add a new dimension to their lives. Employers who want to benefit from this dedicated working potential adjust working conditions to fit women's needs. This is true, for example, with regard to recruitment, creches and running a flexible working day.

Some companies have introduced a recruitment strategy specifically aimed at women over 40 and mothers who wish to return to work. They advertise in local newspapers with an invitation for 'a cup of tea and an informal chat' at a pleasant restaurant or hotel. At the first meeting of this kind in an English town 40 women turned up, and 32 of these were invited to participate in the company's training programme. Previously all of them had been unemployed.

The women are able to work the same number of hours as their children spend at school, and they can also take time off in the school holidays. The gap is filled by students doing vacation work. For this target group the company started its own sales school. A thorough induction course is followed by one day's schooling every five weeks, with the objective not only of training adept sales personnel, but also of building up self-confidence. In this way, the women can gradually be prepared to take on positions of greater responsibility.

Ever more women are choosing to train to more advanced levels. In addition to their qualifications it is then their social competence which comes to the fore in predominantly male leadership teams. This is apparent, for example, in cases where beneath the surface tensions, which might eventually have a negative effect on productivity and morale, need to be brought into the open in good time. After exhaustive research into the subject, the American author Marilyn Loden states in her book, *Feminine Leadership*, that women are better equipped than men to think in totalities when trying to solve problems.

In her book *You Just Don't Understand*, best selling author Deborah Tannen writes:

'If women focus on connexions, they will be motivated to minimize the difference in expertise and be as comprehensible as possible. Since their goal is to maintain the appearance of similarity and equal status, sharing knowledge helps even the score . . . For most women the language of conversation is primarily one of rapport: a way of establishing connexions and negotiating relationships. Emphasis is placed on revealing similarities and likening experiences.'

The negative side of the coin is that women's longing for harmony can be so overwhelming that they don't accept differences. Tannen writes: 'From a young age girls criticise their peers when they try to stand out or appear better than others'.

My own experience of working with both all-female groups and male-dominated management courses suggest that there is a noticeable difference in attitudes and values. Women on lower levels of the hierarchy, in particular, are more open, more interested in inter-human relations, and are less prestige-conscious and more task-orientated than men. But precisely this difference would seem to lessen women's career prospects. To get on, many women therefore adopt male norms and patterns of behaviour.

It is not a question of whether men or women are better managers, but of striking a balance between male and female values. The challenge to women is to focus more on their aims while still retaining their concern, warmth and equality. The challenge to men is to become more closely acquainted with their emotions. The best working environment will be created when there is an even distribution of men and women in all types of positions.

# 3 | Motivation and innovation

In the short run you
can stamp on
people.
In the long run you
pay and pay.

Companies invest billions of pounds in developing new technologies, in automation, and in rationalizing administrations. All of which is necessary. There is, however, always the danger that too radical an economic drive will not only get rid of excess weight, but harm motivation and the working atmosphere into the bargain.

## No qualified staff = no expertise

In the economic debate there is a lot of talk about accumulating capital, but little about creating good growth conditions for people. If a company gets into difficulties, workers are made redundant, and with them also goes their experience. The advantages of rationalization in the short-term often ruin the chances for growth in the long-term.

The construction industry in Germany, for example, undertook a radical reduction in the labour force during the last recession. Now the economy is booming, and they are desperately short of skilled workers. Training is difficult because there are hardly any people left who are qualified to train others, and in some fields the average age of workers is over 50.

It is not only the experience of those who are made redundant which is lost, but also of those who decide to leave of their own free will, even though the company would actually like them to stay. If rumours about redundancies get round there is often a voluntary mass-exodus of employees – and it is always the best who go first. They are quickly lapped up by the competition.

Well qualified experts of the right age easily find new jobs, and are thus the first to desert a sinking ship even though their own positions are not in danger. The space they leave behind can be filled by others, but experts do not grow on trees. The replacements often lack experience and, above all, personal contacts. If the worst comes to the worst, a company may end up recruiting extra overheads while losing orders.

A management consulting firm was busy selling its clients solutions while it was itself suffering from sub-standard leadership. Top management was under the misapprehension that the company's success rate would improve if they really added fuel to the flames of internal competition among the consultants. To this end they introduced an intricate bonus system – 'The winner takes it all, the others go to the wall.' In fact, they achieved the very opposite.

After a while no-one was able to trust anyone else. Everybody tried to steal everybody else's clients, and gradually the working atmosphere became so unbearable that one consultant after the other handed in their notice and started up a new firm. In the end, even the secretaries had had enough of endless arguments as to the number of hours they had spent working for which of the consultants, and followed their particular favourite into his new company. Then the employees in the accounts department could no longer bear the wranglings about how the bonus was to be distributed. By the end of a year there was only one member of the original staff left.

At the outset, money was of no particular concern to the top management. The old consultants had won the company plenty of clients, and new colleagues were employed to take their place. But the consultancy business is based on trust. Who were all these new faces? Nobody wanted to take the risk of spending a lot of money on people who were still 'green'. In the course of the following year, a once very successful firm went into total dissolution.

Employees are not a bunch of heartless money-machines. The better people are qualified, the higher their expectations, not only with regard to salary but also to the emotional climate of the working environment. If people feel they are not appreciated by their superiors they may well decide to hand in their notice. When their experience goes, future profit potential goes with them.

## Motivation during economy drives

Badly-handled reorganization ruins the socio-psychological environment of a company. Inadequate or inaccurate information weakens the trusting relationship between management and the staff. Conflicts poison the atmosphere. If the staff are no longer able to enjoy their work, it is of little account that the multifarious technical systems all function perfectly. It really is worth putting every conceivable effort into maintaining motivation even during slimming campaigns.

People who like things to keep ticking over as they have always done get cold feet when something changes suddenly. Insecurity is fruitful ground for rumour, and fear mobilizes resistance. The way in which changes are implemented determines what the end result will be. If the wrong procedures are chosen, the Managing Director's question, 'How can I cut costs?' can easily turn into a desperate cry of 'Help! I've cut costs according to plan but now everyone is skulking around with long faces. How on earth can I motivate my staff?'

## A small but significant change in attitude

Changing one's attitude is a slow and painful process; changing one's behaviour is all the more so.

People on an ego-trip forget that an organization is more than just the sum of individuals employed. A firm is not a social vacuum. Collaboration produces its own dynamism. If you want to achieve lasting results you have to give as well as take. Measures geared to improving the efficiency of the individual have to be accompanied by actions aimed at strengthening the solidarity of the group.

Managers who quite consciously foster vicious internal competition often fall into a trap. When the process of calculating internal costs takes on ridiculous dimensions, and assistants and secretaries start to make enemies of one another, accusing each other of fiddling the time schedules, this is usually the first sign that something is gravely wrong. When colleagues no longer dare to tell each other about their work for fear of having their ideas or clients whipped from under their noses, all is certainly not well. When nobody has time to get on with their work because they are too busy trying to find out what is happening behind the scenes, and who has been forming secret alliances with whom, at some stage this will be revealed in turnover. When different departments or subsidiaries of a company are all fighting for the same clients, the overall net profit will be zero.

For these reasons it is imperative that managers acquire a basic knowledge of human psychology. The art of motivation lies in releasing emotional energies, and this requires sensitivity and patience. The objective is a small but significant change in the attitude of superiors towards their staff. Then the staff, in turn, will also change their attitudes towards their bosses. You will only ever get as good as you give.

24

# Motivation factors

Motivation is a driving force. If you want to motivate people you have to know something about their motives and satisfy their needs – but what are their needs?

I once carried out an investigation of motivating factors. In response to the question 'What motivates you?', more than 60% gave answers related to satisfying socio-psychological needs: feedback, a feeling of belonging, openness, honesty, credibility, trust, fairness, consideration, responsibility, participation.

About 20% of the answers were concerned with satisfying intellectual needs: self-fulfilment, interesting and varied tasks, challenges.

Only 10% of answers quoted material incentives.

At 1% the quality of the physical space in which people have to work is of little significance. Of course, this does not mean that employees like working in noisy factories or offices with poor lighting and yellowing wallpaper, but when the physical working environment is satisfactory, further improvements only make a negligible impression on productivity. Instead of building palatial offices, management should concern themselves with their employees' emotional needs, and devote more time to in-service training.

Employees consider high demands on themselves an incentive. When asked to describe in their own words what makes work interesting I was told, for example:

- 'The work has to be such that I have to make a bit of extra effort.'
- 'I want to be stretched. Plenty of work. Creativity. Imagination.'
- 'It has to be a challenge, demanding more of me than usual.'
- 'Tasks should be difficult and comprehensive.'
- 'I have to be able to test myself, whether I can manage something and how quickly.'

# Good leadership = not killing motivation

On their first day at work most people are motivated. In the course of time however, the conditions at the place of work cause them to lose their enthusiasm. The meaning of good leadership is to prevent the staff from losing their motivation.

Unfortunately, there are still managers who think that it is not worth the effort to take the needs of their staff into account. Only very few companies and public service authorities bother to draw up a systematic overview of their employees' training, experience and abilities. Many people feel that they are unable to make full use of their potential.

Indifference on the part of superiors eventually results in an attitude of 'you can get on with it on your own' amongst the staff, and dropping productivity. People are bored with their work, either because they receive too little attention or because the regular tasks fall short of their qualifications. The demands are not high enough.

Dissatisfaction with one's own conditions of work can simmer below the surface for years without a manager noticing anything, especially as many employees are unwilling to draw attention to themselves. They want 'Things to change' without being able to state clearly what it is they really want. The reason for this might be resignation ('There's no point'), fear of punishment ('The boss is sitting in the driving seat and might leave me standing at the next traffic lights'), or lack of self-confidence ('I suppose I'm not good enough'). Very few people consider that the staff also have the right to make demands on their superiors.

While many employees consider high demands to be an incentive, the boss often gives them the cold shoulder. Their desire for more responsibility is turned down with the comment that someone has to get their hands dirty.

## Motivation eases reorganization

Motivation eases reorganization. In reply to the question, 'When a company is being reorganized, employees often feel discontented. What are the reasons for such a negative attitude towards innovation?', not even a full quarter of the answers are indicative of a lack of flexibility. All the others reveal a need for more information and security. For example:

- 'I want to know what is supposed to happen and why.'
- 'I want to know to what extent I am going to be affected personally.'
- 'I want to be able to keep control of the situation and participate in the reorganization of my job.'
- 'I want to be sure that I am going to be able to cope with the new aspects of the job.'

Also, in response to the question 'What can the management do in order to motivate the staff to treat change as an opportunity rather than a threat?', most of the answers were concerned with more information and participation. For example:

- 'My superiors ought to explain to me why the reorganization is necessary.'
- 'The management ought to integrate the staff better in the reorganization process so that they feel as though they are involved.'
- 'Thorough in-service training so that the changes become old hat and the staff don't have to be afraid of new developments.'
- 'We have to put the emphasis on in-service training – preferably by introducing a system of remuneration which reflects the will to adjust.'

# Part II—Material incentives

# 4 | The role of incentives

Material incentives can of course play a part in encouraging people to perform at work. But their role must be seen in the context of the whole range of motivating factors. This chapter looks at some of the issues associated with money-based rewards.

## Systems of remuneration

One of the main challenges to companies is to develop systems of remuneration which motivate people. The less someone earns the more important the size of their salary becomes. An unemployed person with debts has but one thought: how can I get hold of more money? And low-paid workers are dependent on every extra penny they can get. The more people earn and the more they identify with what they are doing, the less the relative importance of money becomes. Its place is taken by recognition for achievement and freedom of action, i.e. the possibility to influence what will happen.

As the competition for well-qualified staff becomes more fierce, material incentives alone will fail to attract the right people. For those with no pressing financial worries a sense of well-being is more important than money, and the factors which influence well-being are human contact, mutual trust, and the feeling of being appreciated and treated fairly. Furthermore, the opportunity to learn something new and to realize one's potential help to create a positive feeling.

In cooperation with the Boston Consulting Group, the German publication *manager magazin* carried out a survey of research and development activities among the three leading industrialized nations: Japan, the USA, and Germany. One of the main questions was 'Who is best at management?' Among other things, the findings of the questionnaire reveal that both American and Japanese top managers judge their research and development staff to be highly motivated. On a 7-point scale, the USA registered 5.2 and Japan 6.2. In response to the question 'What actually motivated people?', the answer was unequivocal: more information and participation in the decision-making process at the top of the list, while a higher salary came right at the bottom.

**Material incentives are not attractive**
**How motivation factors rate**

| Scale | | Motivation factor |
|-------|-------|-------------------|
| US | Japan | |
| 1 | 1 | Clearer strategic directives |
| 2 | 3 | More information |
| 3 | 2 | Greater participation in project planning |
| 4 | 6 | Less organizational bureaucracy |
| 5 | 4 | More openness to ideas from outside |
| 6 | 5 | Less routine work |
| 7 | 8 | More in-service training |
| 8 | 7 | Better prospects for promotion |
| 9 | 9 | Higher salaries |

*Source: 'manager magazin', November 1988.*

Positive incentives which satisfy both the intellectual and emotional needs of staff are more effective than negative motivation in the form of threats or punishment.

# Money as a motivating factor

Everybody wants to earn more. Money is frequently the number one talking-point at work, especially in firms where an employee's value is judged according to sales statistics. As salaries get higher, so too do expectations. Need knows no boundaries: spend, spend, spend. It doesn't matter how much arrives in your account each month, it is never enough. And there is always somebody who is earning more than you are. This causes discontent.

Salaries are significant in more than one respect:

- A salary guarantees a livelihood and is thus an incentive to work.

- The size of salary indicates an employee's status, not only in the internal company hierarchy but also in relation to neighbours, friends and other groups in society.
- An increase in salary is confirmation of success at your job.
- Last but not least, a pay-rise may compensate for a life devoid of feeling and deeper emotional involvement with others.

## Good pay is important, a good working atmosphere is even more crucial

Money is not as large a motivating factor as is generally assumed. If one's salary is high enough to cover the mortgage, an adequate wardrobe, any existing debts, and the occasional meal out, and if, on top of this, there is still enough left over for the annual holiday, an increase in salary has little effect on labour-input. Of course, nobody is actually going to turn down an offer of extra cash, but a higher income soon becomes a habit and is taken for granted.

What encourages people to make greater effort is much more closely related to personal well-being, the climate of human relationships, and the type of work involved. A good atmosphere, interesting work, and real prospects for personal development attract well-qualified staff. It is when these factors are lacking that staff start leafing through the job advertisements – then, of course, they choose jobs which offer higher salaries.

Motivation is linked first and foremost to factors other than money. Conversely, a high salary does not automatically ensure that people enjoy their work. The good news for management is they can do a great deal to increase their employees' motivation without it costing them a penny.

## Demands for a higher salary also represent a call for attention

If salaries are only a secondary motivating factor, why do people go on strike for higher wages? The ones who shout the loudest are not normally those on social security who are afraid that they might lose their houses because they cannot afford the interest rates. Indeed, it is often people with good qualifications and high salaries who send wages spiralling.

Striking for more money is also a call for a higher status and greater consideration. People on strike want to draw attention to themselves: 'We are carrying out an important role in society. Just look how everything breaks down if we withhold our labour. Give us the attention we deserve. If you don't want to do it of your own free will, we'll just have to make you.'

33

Very few people are able to admit openly that they feel they have been passed over, ignored, neglected and under-estimated. It is easier to talk about money than feelings. Thus they try to account for their dissatisfaction with inadequate remuneration.

**Payment as a status symbol**

The size of salary also indicates status within a firm's internal hierarchy. Every individual compares his salary with that of his colleagues, and many consider themselves to be under-paid. Civil servants compare their salaries with those paid by industry. Academics think that they earn too little by comparison with labourers. When top British managers see what their American counterparts earn, they feel like poor relations. Paying higher salaries to people who are already earning a lot of money does not increase their motivation. They will simply go on comparing themselves with those who earn more.

What is decisive is that pay is understood to be fair both with regard to one's own input and that of others. Thus it is important that staff are involved in determining the criteria which form the basis for pay agreements and promotions. Is it economic success, expertise, or the number of years one has been working for the company which carry the greatest weight? How do personal characteristics such as cooperation and initiative rate? Who receives the greater reward, people who use their elbows or people who manage to create a caring and trusting environment? How much advantage does the power-crazy manipulator claim for himself by fawning to his superiors and distancing himself from his colleagues and subordinates?

The criteria for pay-rises must be known and accepted by everybody if a situation is to be avoided in which the staff waste their energies on self-pity or sabotage because they feel they are being treated unfairly.

Staff with similar tasks and comparable input should receive roughly the same salary. Frustration about salary discrimination can cause people to hand in their notice, even though the size of the salary itself is not unsatisfactory. For the same work women frequently earn less than men.

A public service employee handed in her notice because she found her job too boring. In industry she immediately earned far more per annum. She was proud and satisfied. After a while, however, she discovered that her male colleagues were earning considerably more for exactly the same job. Some of them did not even have such good qualifications as she did. The employee became dissatisfied although, objectively, she was still earning a great deal more than in her old job. When her subsequent attempt to achieve parity fell on deaf ears she handed in her notice. She was extremely angry – not because she did not earn enough, but because her male colleagues earned more for the same work. The keyword here is fairness.

## A pay-rise as confirmation of professional success

Most people want to develop and make the best of themselves. Success at work satisfies the need for status and recognition. The form which such confirmation takes might be promotion, a new title, or a raise in salary.

On the other hand, it is very bad for motivation to continue doing exactly the same year-in, year-out on precisely the same scale of salary. This is a fate suffered by many women who lack training. Managers should also give a chance to those who are not ambitious to proceed to managerial positions. Greater responsibility and more variation in carrying-out everyday tasks are a form of horizontal advancement.

Confirmation of professional success does not necessarily need to take the form of higher pay. Any company can create its own rituals and symbols. An encouraging word from the boss might be worth its weight in gold.

The magazine *Management Wissen* reported on a German survey on how people in a research environment react to career stagnation. The staff were divided into three groups:

– Those who had been promoted and were successful.
– Those who had experienced a variety of fields through job rotation, but had not been promoted.
– Those who had come to a standstill in their careers.

It is hardly surprising that those who had 'made it' were most satisfied. This group spent more hours at the working place, achieved better results, showed more initiative, and communicated better both with colleagues and superiors in their own and other departments.

By contrast, the group which had experienced a variety of fields, but which had not been promoted, demonstrated the same patterns of behaviour as the poor devils in group three whose careers had stagnated totally. Their psychological state included discontent, diminishing enthusiasm for work, little contact with others, loneliness, apathy, strain, stress, anxiety, and depression. On the physical side they suffered from breathing difficulties, high blood-pressure, ulcers and heart attacks.

The stress caused by people not being able to realize their potential and stagnating in their professional development is more difficult for goal-getters to bear than the stress ensuing from overwork.

Interesting and varied tasks on their own, for example in the form of job rotation, are not enough to increase motivation to any extent. The survey cited did, however, reveal that staff who are not only given interesting tasks but also their superior's attention without actually being promoted develop the same attitudes and feelings as their colleagues who have achieved career success: greater commitment and willingness to work, as well as better communication with others.

Once again, this confirms the theory that taking notice of people is the key to motivating them.

## Money as compensation for a life devoid of emotion

Why do people always want more money when everybody knows that money does not guarantee you happiness? Money can compensate for a life devoid of genuine human contact.

Someone who is always working hard and earns a considerable amount of money often has no time to enjoy the fruits of his labour. Many managers have only a few, and sometimes no close friends at all. Family life has frequently been sacrificed to career: divorce and the concomitant loss of the children is quite consciously accepted by many as the price to be paid for the advancement of their careers. The second marriage often hangs by a silken thread, especially if the wife has the audacity to wish to see her husband relaxing occasionally. Purchasing luxury gifts then signifies the final attempt to save such an endangered marriage.

A busy manager wanted to conciliate his wife who was complaining that he was never at home. As proof of his love he bought her a luxury yacht. It was a well-meaning attempt to reintroduce a little romance into their tedious married life. Unfortunately, it was a long time since the two of them had talked to each other about anything. He had no idea what the person he lived under the same roof with actually wanted, and he did not take the trouble to ask. Later, he came to regret this: his wife had an aversion to water and hated boats.

Constantly striving for more money can also be seen as compensation for stress and discontent at work. A well-paid computer specialist explains her desire for a higher salary as follows:

'I don't find my work very satisfying. The working atmosphere is awful and I don't feel at ease with my colleagues. I work long hours so I don't have much free time, and hardly any contacts outside work. I have neglected my friends and my body. In the evening I'm simply too tired to force myself to go to gymnastics. I don't have time to join any clubs or a political party. To make up for all this at least I want to earn enough money to pay my debts, have a nice home and a decent pension.'

## Not by bread alone

Man cannot live by bread alone. A feeling of well-being at work counts for much more than money.

From an historical point of view we are in a unique situation. Throughout the centuries man has had to work just to survive. Now, for the first time, he can allow himself the luxury – at least this is the case for those of us with good qualifications and secure employment in our part of the world – of taking emotional and intellectual needs into account.

I should like to draw two conclusions from what has been discussed to-date:

- Management should not rely solely on material incentives, but should carry out an internal survey to discover what motivates the staff in their company, and what fails to motivate them. The appendix gives a questionnaire which can be used for this purpose. The questions should be answered anonymously. It is of no use if the findings end up in the bottom of a drawer. Take the risk and discuss them openly, and then put any good suggestions into practice.

  A high degree of motivation not only contributes to the individual's feeling of well-being, but also has positive economic implications: companies with shared visions and a motivated staff have increased profit and productivity, and have reduced the accident rate and absenteeism. The elements which make work enjoyable tend to be independent of the size of salary. It does not cost very much to motivate staff.
- Trade unions, which are supposed to represent the interests of the workforce, would be well advised to fight more actively for their members' non-material needs. We spend so many hours at our workplace that it is not a matter of indifference whether we end up a bundle of nerves and get turned-out prior to retirement-age or whether we can retain our creativity and joy in life well on into old age. Well-being at work is the precondition for enjoying leisure.

As long as everything revolves around money, employers and employees will have opposing interests. By contrast, motivation arising from recognition, participation and self-realization creates a basis for setting common goals. In the face of such important global, European and demographic challenges, the time is ripe for employers and employees to realize that they are all in the same boat.

# Part III—Communication as a motivator

# 5 | Communication within the company

Open communication means that information flows freely from top to bottom, from bottom to top, and right the way through an organization. Open communication means that reciprocal feedback can be passed on in an atmosphere of trust. Open communication means that people are interested in each other, take notice of each other, and show each other respect.

Employees want to know what they are supposed to do and why, what their superiors expect of them, and how far what is going on in other departments and outside the company is of relevance to their own work.

It is an important managerial responsibility to ensure the free flow of information within the company. The manager always sets an example. His private attitudes and public behaviour indicate to the staff whether they can dare to be open with him. Thus it is essential that the manager's words and deeds are not at odds with one another.

If a manager fails to pass on sufficient information the employees should take the initiative themselves and, if necessary, ask him to elucidate:

- 'Is there anything else I ought to know?'
- 'Could I bring up this matter with you again. I should like to be sure that I have understood you properly.'
- 'When might I call you back in case there are any other questions?'

## Uncertainty produces fear

**41** The need for information is particularly marked before, during and following periods of great upheaval such as organizational restructuring or company mergers. When the devil you know disappears it is entirely unclear what the devil you don't might be up to.

Uncertainty is fruitful ground for rumour, and causes staff to start worrying about failing in their new role, or even losing their job.

The greater the uncertainty, the less the productivity. Inadequate, delayed or implausible information starts rumours going, and even if the management tries to keep things in the dark, a few bits and pieces always come to light. Staff group together and start speculating what might happen. If one person thinks that this or that solution may have been found, the second person tells the third person that this is what has been decided. Staff end up wasting enormous amounts of time and energy trying to find out what is going on. Their work takes a back seat.

In this situation employees feel threatened and disorientated. Many are afraid of having the ground cut from under their feet:

- 'What's going to happen next?'
- 'What is this reorganization going to mean for me, personally?'
- 'Who knows where it'll all end?'

What is at stake are accrued rights and privileges, status and prestige. A transfer to another department or town smacks of demotion when the management presents those affected with a *fait accompli*, and does not allow them to participate in the layout of the future workplace:

- 'Why me?'
- 'Doesn't the boss like me?'
- 'Is this what I get for opening my mouth about this or that?'
- 'Hasn't my work been satisfactory?'

Particularly when new techniques are being introduced, older employees fear that they are going to be edged out by younger colleagues:

- 'What'll happen when I can't keep up any more?'
- 'I'll never manage that!'
- 'What'll happen to me then?'

Just imagine the case of an experienced cashier of advanced years whom everybody respects. One day he comes into the office and finds a brand new computer on his desk. But no-one has thought to initiate him into the secrets of electronic data-processing. At a stroke, the experience of a lifetime is made worthless. Where he used to be an authority he is now just a has-been. His job is taken on by a younger colleague with data-processing experience. Psychiatrists' waiting rooms are full of such people who have been left behind by technological advance.

Of course, each individual employee is responsible for his or her personal and professional development. Staff should be willing to participate in in-service training, and be flexible enough to adapt to new situations. Undoubtedly, some will be too phlegmatic to bother, or only realize when it is too late. But it is also the responsibility of the management to make sure that they are informed about future developments, and that they have the opportunity to train accordingly. In this way they will be less anxious about the introduction of new technologies and, in its turn, this will mean that their human resources can be used more purposefully in the interest of the company.

Fear of losing one's job is the worst nightmare. Terms like 'rationalization', 'automation', 'cutting costs' and 'remaining competitive' are often just euphemisms for making people redundant.

A bank clerk describes his unease as follows:

'I get worried when I think about increasing automation in banking. Being responsible for this field means having the ground cut from under my feet. If the number of customers using cash dispensers keep increasing I'll end up being superfluous. Banking isn't the secure employment it used to be.'

Uncertainty and anxiety form the basis for irrational reactions. A considerable amount of resistance to change has its origins in insecurity.

## Information encourages security and trust

Keeping people informed encourages security and trust – providing the management of the company is considered credible on the strength of past experience.

If redundancies are unavoidable companies should accept their social responsibility, and help their superfluous staff to find alternative employment by ensuring that they are an attractive proposition for other companies.

An electronics company placed the following advertisement in the newspaper:

'Are you on the lookout for competent staff? The development of the economy in the last year in combination with the radical change in our technology has meant that we require a far smaller labour-force. We thus have a number of employees who are looking for alternative employment.

We will provide you with an overview of the theoretical and practical background at the earliest opportunity. We are prepared to release staff immediately so that the new employer is not required to wait until the standard period of notice has elapsed.

30% lower payload! On top of this we offer to cover 30% of your new employee's current basic salary in the first 12 months – for those over 50 in the first 24 months. This offer is valid for those who are taken on in permanent employment. You can choose staff from a variety of different fields of work.'

## Information at the first opportunity

To remain credible during times of difficulty it is essential to build up a trusting relationship with employees, the media, and others affected by the company's affairs – before the disaster is a fact. Money spent on image polishing is not wasted if the self-image coincides with reality.

In times of upheaval employees should be informed what is going on at the first opportunity. The management of a company often forget that they have a lead over the rest of the staff both in knowledge and time. The managers have already discussed various suggestions, and had time to think about the implications even before the staff have heard about the problem.

Staff also need time to get used to changes. The sooner they are informed what is supposed to be happening, the easier it is for them to prepare themselves psychologically.

The management should always speak to their own employees before they reveal their news to the media. Far too often the workforce has to read the newspapers to learn about the changes taking place in their own company.

Keeping people informed is not a one-off affair. A single round of information about the company's objectives is simply not enough. Keep the flow of information going constantly, and encourage your staff to think along with you. Include them in the internal discussion, and listen to their ideas – but from the word go, not from the night before the innovations are about to be introduced.

## Information on what is going to happen

Inform people what is supposed to be happening. Be honest and concrete. According to an Ashanti proverb, 'One falsehood spoils a thousand truths', and you can certainly assume that the short-term tactical advantage to be gained from telling half-truths will soon be done away with by weakening the basis for trust in the long-term. Detailed information makes unfounded opposition null and void. Think about answers to the following questions:

- What is supposed to happen?
- Who is going to be affected, and how are they going to be affected?
- When is it going to happen?
- Who is supposed to comment on it?
- Who is supposed to make the final decision?
- What consequences will the decision have, and for whom?
- Who has to be informed about what?

## Information on why it is going to happen

Informing people what is going to happen must be quickly followed by information about why. Companies spend millions on advertising in order to convince potential customers. Equally important is internal marketing in order to convince the company's own employees.

Even if, on an extremely busy day, a manager simply forgets to pass on information to his staff, the effect is the same as if it had been withheld on purpose. Employees interpret the omission as the boss's indifference, and respond with distrust and a lack of interest in their work:

- 'If no-one's going to bother to pay any regard to me, why should I go out of my way for the firm?'
- 'When nobody dare open their mouth there must be something a bit fishy somewhere.'

Frequently, the reasons for a defensive attitude towards innovation stem from a feeling of being totally insignificant in the eyes of the manager, and not being taken seriously.

Take the trouble to convince your staff about what is happening, and present your ideas in a psychologically sound manner. Positive arguments are more motivating than threats. For example:

- The planned innovations offer you the following possibilities, advantages and positive perspectives.
- Changes, which are in the interest of the company, contribute to guaranteeing employment.
- The loss of x jobs is unavoidable for xyz reasons. But the management has made the following provisions for those who choose to leave or are made redundant.

- The management has called in an external consultant who will help those made redundant to cope with their situation by talking through the psychological difficulties, and also by assisting them in the search for new employment.
- The restructuring will mean that staff are given more interesting tasks. The management is offering xyz opportunities for in-service training.
- The introduction of a more advanced electronic data system will help you to do your work more quickly and clearly. It will also allow you better access to important information.
- Your field of responsibility will be widened to include xyz. This will be reflected in an increase in salary.
- We can offer you xyz opportunities for training.
- We envisage the following measures with regard to personal development.
- By comparison with the old, the new regime has the following advantages in relation to efficiency and productivity.
- Your transfer to the new department should be taken as a compliment. You have precisely the abilities we require for the post there.
- In our experience most people find it stimulating to learn something new. We guarantee you thorough job-familiarization.

## Information channels

There is a wealth of possible channels of information:

- Messages via the data processing network.
- Internal company radio.
- Videos.
- Circulars and other written information.
- Personal contact and attention.

### Electronic data network

Information from the computer is most suitable for passing on facts and news. The advantage of a computer network is that a large number of people can be reached very quickly. The disadvantage is that the information often only flows in one direction, and is unavoidably impersonal.

### Internal company radio

Internal company radio can be very entertaining, but remains a typical one-way communication system.

## Videos

Even with videos, information only flows in one direction. Apart from this, the production of professional videos is fairly expensive. Thus it can be tempting just to produce a single standard video for differing purposes and target groups which then frequently fails to hit the target altogether. Those watching do not feel it has anything to do with them, and may even reject the message completely.

The women's group of a political party organized a conference on environmental protection. Within the framework of the conference they asked whether they might visit the plant of a company successful in the field of pollution-control technology. The group was courteously received by the head of information, who invited them to watch a video about the company and their products. The film showed the managing director talking to a male management consultant. They compared the team spirit in the company with that of a football team, and used language, similes and examples exclusively geared to male fields of experience. During the 20 minutes the film lasted not a single woman was featured. It was a film about men, for men which was shown to the women.

Quite apart from the fact that the women felt provoked by the portrayal of environmental protection as a purely male domain, they were taken aback by only being presented with company reality in the form of a video. A personal word from the director or a discussion with some of the staff would have been more convincing.

Communication via video can be compared with talking to an answering machine. The motivation to speak is weakened because the other side remains dumb. Without a response there can be no inspiration. Many people hang up when they hear a recorded voice at the other end of the telephone line. Similarly, many people switch off mentally when they are supposed to take in information passively from their superiors appearing on a screen.

The more technically competent a video is, the greater the distance from company reality. Many expensive and aesthetically sophisticated videos do no more for the staff than bring on a fit of yawning and strengthen the feeling of 'them up there and us down here'.

Interactive video allows staff to search for a specific type of information on what is happening in and around the company. This satisfies the need for information on facts, but it doesn't satisfy the need for personal contact and attention.

Videos may well be justified as one part of a comprehensive programme for disseminating information, but they can never be a substitute for face-to-face dialogue.

## Circulars and other written information

Circulars and other written information are often filed away unread in the hope of having time to read them at a later stage. By the time this stage comes, if ever, they are usually hopelessly out of date.

It says little for human understanding to inform people about impending redundancy by posting an information sheet on the noticeboard. In connection with subjects with such far-reaching consequences, personal contact is essential.

Many managers justify their actions by saying that they have no time to speak to their staff personally. Constantly having too much to do is, however, frequently an unconscious means of evading difficult situations in the field of human relationships. In his heart of hearts, the manager is afraid of open communication and coming to terms with his own feelings, and thus keeps his staff at a distance. The only person he harms by doing this is himself. He is losing contact with reality, and from there it is not a long step to taking the wrong decisions.

There are similarities with marriage: if the partners stop discussing unpleasant things with one another openly, communication gradually breaks down completely. More and more issues are put under taboo because they might evoke forbidden thoughts and feelings. Finally, the partners end up only talking about superficial things, and discover too late how far apart they have grown. The final break is then the only solution left to them.

## Personal contact and attention

However much information is passed on there will always be complaints that it is not enough. A call for more information is often nothing more than a call for more attention, openness, credibility, trust and, above all, personal contact:

- 'Say openly where we're supposed to be going, don't try to hush things up.'
- 'If only my boss would tell me honestly what the changes will actually mean for me.'
- 'Just talk to each of us a little bit more.'

The staff say 'information', i.e. the facts required in a given situation, but really mean 'attention', i.e. the satisfaction of an emotional need. The management of a company needs to be aware of this fine difference. The most up-to-date computer network with daily messages to each individual employee can never be an adequate substitute for the immediate contact between managers and their staff.

A face-to-face discussion is the best way of disseminating information. Managers and staff should always talk to one another rather than trying to communicate by way of closely-written sheets of A4 paper. Of course, the Managing Director does not have the time to wander along the corridors all day long enquiring into the health of people's ailing grandmothers, but this does not mean that he should never show his face on the lower floors at all. He can always talk to his staff in groups.

The immediate boss is in a better position to cultivate close contact with his staff. Structured forms of cooperation guarantee effective participation. The deeper the mutual trust and the better the personal contact, the easier it is for the department or group to dispense with formal information channels such as meetings and written directives.

Obviously, not every single item needs to be discussed with the Managing Director personally, but everybody should have someone with whom he or she can discuss matters. Openness about what is going on within the company should also extend to the lower-ranking employees. The caretaker and the cleaning staff are also keen to identify with their workplace, and this includes information about what is happening. A secretary might be entrusted with important information destined for others.

**Informal networks**

In any workplace there is an informal network of contacts:

- Who talks to whom?
- Who meets whom outside working hours?
- Who supports whom?

Informal networks play an important role in the run-up to decision-making. Who prefers which solution, who supports whom, and who will be promoted is often discussed over a pint. The official meetings merely confirm what those within the network have decided in advance.

If you want to belong to the informal network you have to prove your social competence. Elbows and intrigues do not pay in the long run. If you set a trap for others you may well fall in yourself – perhaps not today or tomorrow, but sooner or later it is inevitable. Many bankrupt companies, which thrived in former years, engineered their own demise in internal battles for power. Their difficulties in the market were merely the straw that broke the camel's back.

To achieve objectives it is important for the manager to know as much as possible about the social environment in which the company functions:

- What are the interests, opinions and wishes of those affected by decisions? Have I taken them into account? What can I do to help them?
- Will my decision make difficulties for anyone? What can I do to lessen the pain?
- What other points could lead to conflict?
- Who is powerful enough to counter my ideas? What reasons could they have for using that power?
- Who is the opinion leader? How can I win him over to my cause?
- Whose agreement do I require otherwise?
- How can I find reliable allies?

The greater the dependence on others, the more important it is to have a good relationship with superiors and colleagues. Clever managers realize that they are dependent on their staff. They understand that 'the only way to get your outcome is to see that everyone else involved gets his or her outcome, too . . . because the others involved become your allies, not your saboteurs' (Genie Z. Laborde, *Influencing with Integrity*).

## A questionnaire for examining information needs

- How satisfied are you with the internal dissemination of information?
- Do you have any suggestions for improvement? What are they?
- What sort of information do you need to do your job? How much? How frequently?
- Are you given too much or unnecessary information? What? From whom? What do you think about the timing? Is it too early, too late or just right?
- Do you yourself have access to information which you are supposed to pass on to the others? What? To whom?
- Have you been told to pass on information to others which they do not seem to need? Which items? Volume? Frequency?
- Are there unclear forms or unsuitable routines for reporting back in your field of work? Which?

– Do you have a clear idea about the sort of cases in which you pass on information in a written form and those in which you contact someone personally? Which?

# 6 | The power of feedback

Open communication serves to guarantee quality. The travelling salesman and the bank clerk at the counter are the first to hear customers' complaints, and they can decide whether or not to pass them on to the section responsible. This assumes, however, that they are able to point out mistakes and make suggestions without having fear of recrimination, and furthermore, that their superiors take the time to listen to them.

Many painful measures ensuing from reorganization might have been avoided had the management been aware of what was going on at grassroot level. Many accidents and catastrophes might have been prevented had the words of warning reached the management earlier.

A British mine was renowned for frequent accidents. An investigation of the causes revealed that the miners hardly had any contact at all with their superiors. The flow of information only ran from top to bottom. After the management had agreed to regular meetings with the workforce, the number of accidents fell drastically.

In the global race for first place in new technologies, research and development determine who comes in first. Yet success is not only a product of technological know-how and financial strength, but also of teamwork and communication.

In the *manager magazin* survey referred to earlier, the findings revealed:

'The weak points . . . do not lie in a lack of planning and control . . . Rather it is problems related to communication and coordination which are responsible for the lack of efficiency in research and development management.

52

Objectives which have been set may not be achieved because they are not formulated clearly or because they are not introduced into the organization systematically. There is not sufficient feedback and the coordination with other sections (especially marketing) does not function properly' (*manager magazin*, October 1988).

European high-tech companies such as Siemens, Philips, Olivetti, Bull, etc. are fighting for survival. The Japanese are always first and cheaper. This is even more true for the automobile industry. Toyota particularly is causing headaches for Mercedes, BMW, Volkswagen, Fiat, Peugeot, Renault, General Motors, Ford and Chrysler. One of the secrets for Toyota's success is teamwork and open communication. Managers and staff talk to each other. Workers are encouraged to make improvement suggestions, and are empowered to stop the whole assembly line whenever necessary. As a result they feel responsible for their work, and dedicated to high quality. This saves costs.

The main difference between European and Japanese companies is the way people treat each other. Japanese managers listen to the workers, and regard them as their most important source of information. They discuss with each other how quality and production methods can be further improved. To stimulate teamwork and mutual understanding, each junior manager is supposed to work two months in the sales department and on the assembly line. The appreciation of quality work is also reflected in the fact that new Toyota workers get 380 hours' training in various fields, and afterwards are paid a salary comparable with those in middle management. No wonder that both American and British workers prefer to work for Japanese companies rather than for their fellow countrymen.

# The need for response

Man is a social being involved in constant interaction with his environment, reacting to the impulses it offers him. What do the family, friends, the boss and colleagues think about me? Do they like me or do they look down at me? I love those who love me. I will stand up for those who show me that I mean something to them.

Giving feedback means showing interest. If a manager cares for his employees he enhances their sense of their own value: 'He is not indifferent to me. I belong.' A feeling of belonging is a fundamental motivating factor.

Whether or not the individual's needs for recognition is satisfied within the company directly influences productivity and economic performance. Everybody is supposed to be working towards a common goal, but this assumes that everybody knows what this goal is and identifies with it. If the individual interprets his own job as being an important facet of the whole, the stronger will be his feeling that his job is essential if the goal is to be achieved. Feedback from his boss helps him to recognize that his personal input is an important element in the common collaboration of all.

Just how important identification is can be seen in the following example:

When I was translating this book into German I employed an assistant at a good salary. I identified very closely with the project, worked long hours, and concentrated hard. After all, I was involved in realizing my own ideas and interests. But for my assistant it was a job much like any other. By the end of the agreed contract period I had translated 70 pages while she had only managed 30. It makes an enormous difference whether you are motivated or only doing something for the money.

The number of hours spent at the workplace is often less significant than the way in which they are spent. Is time taken up with trivialities, or is it used efficiently and purposefully?

A response encourages greater achievement. Both positive and negative feedback are important. Recognition for a job well done leads to further involvement, and constructive criticism can inspire people to take themselves to task and develop their own potential. But it is essential to choose the right form of expression. A put-down can destroy someone, whereas criticism clothed in encouragement can help the person concerned to learn from his mistakes.

Many people find it more difficult to praise than to criticize. This is a result of early childhood experience. During childhood it always falls to parents, teachers and other adults to distribute praise. In a fit of rage a small child might shout and scream swear words at people without the world coming to an end. Usually the child's environment reacts more or less tolerantly: 'He's only little and doesn't know what he's saying.' But imagine what would happen to the power structures within the family if the child suddenly had the audacity to say to his father: 'There's a good boy', or 'You really did that very well.' On top of all, it would be grotesque, and the adults would probably laugh out loud. Thus the child gradually learns that praise only comes from above; as an adult he has to fight against his reluctance to praise someone from a position of inferiority. An ordinary member of staff could not possibly dare to give his boss an encouraging pat on the back.

A weak manager who secretly doubts his own ability is mean with praise and recognition. He simply cannot cope. He does not possess the necessary self-confidence to evaluate his staff. The same is true for people who are afraid of coming to terms with their own feelings. When they meet someone who is challenging their adopted attitudes and beliefs, they often react with a put-down, or even attack the other person.

Insecure people often mistrust their own instincts. They are worried about not having the knowledge or experience to make a correct judgement. They fear being dismissed as blue-eyed or uncritical if they praise someone's accomplishment: 'Just imagine if I were the only one to say "excellent". I'd make a fool of myself. The others would think I didn't have any grounds for comparison. I think I'd better go easy on the praise.'

I observe this phenomenon during my seminars. Usually the participants write 'excellent' or 'very good' in their course-evaluation, but there are those who just note 'good'. By encouraging them to sign their names under their evaluation sheets I have discovered that those who are most insecure in themselves are the ones who award the worst marks.

At the end of one seminar I swapped places with the manager so that she could chair the closing summary while I sat amongst the participants. My neighbour had crossed 'good' on his evaluation sheet. Then, one of the participants who counted as an opinion leader announced 'That was a very good course', at which my neighbour altered his own evaluation to 'very good'.

I also receive written commentaries such as:

'The course was terrific, the lecturer very able and pleasant. I have to admit, however, that this was the first time I had been to a course of this kind and therefore I do not have any basis for comparison. It is always difficult to write "excellent" about the person running the course. But it was difficult to find fault with your presentation. Due to these diffuse feelings I wrote "very good".'

On top of this lack of confidence in his own judgement, an insecure person experiences other people's achievements as a personal threat, not only to his position but also to his self-esteem. He interprets the fact that others are good as confirmation of his own inferiority. He thinks in black and white: 'either (them) – or (me)', and 'winners and losers'. His inner doubts cloud his understanding that there is 'strength in numbers'. In the long run it is only possible to achieve good results with each other, not against each other. The ability to pass on positive feedback is founded on inner strength.

# A lack of response kills commitment

Everybody knows that feedback is important. In spite of this, managers frequently have more than enough to do without it. In reply to the question in my survey 'Do you feel that your

"I never hear a word from my boss. Instead of a Christmas present I'd really prefer a few personal words and some comments about my work so that I knew where I stood."

*An employee's Christmas wish*

immediate boss takes sufficient notice of your work?', only 48% answered 'yes'. More than half of all employees get too little response. Men, by the way, get more attention than women. If you break down the figures according to sex, 53% of men feel that their bosses take enough interest in their work, while only 44% of women feel the same. The survey also reveals that staff in higher positions receive more feedback than those lower down the hierarchy.

Here are some typical answers:

– 'Since I never hear anything positive or negative I really haven't the least idea.'
– 'I feel as though I'm working in a vacuum without my boss taking any particular interest in what I'm doing.'
– 'I never find out whether my boss is happy with my work or not.'
– 'The boss couldn't care less about my work.'

A lack of response signals indifference, contempt and punishment. Motivation dies.

A large firm of management consultants wanted to develop a new concept. Through a third party the Managing Director contracted two consultants to draw up a new model. He did not speak to them himself, and did not offer any further explanation. Since the consultants were often away on business they used the weekends to work out a joint proposal. They put in a lot of unpaid overtime so as to be finished in time. As the Managing Director was rarely, if ever, available they sent the project through the internal mail.

They never heard another word from the Managing Director. His confidant who had passed on the job in the first place fobbed them off with evasive answers, implying that something or other was presumably not as the Managing Director had expected, but he was unable to specify what or why.

The consultants were frustrated, feeling that they had wasted their free time for nothing, and within a few months both of them left the firm. The reason for handing in their notice was not this one isolated episode, but rather the fact that this experience was typical of the behaviour cultivated in the company. They left because they did not feel happy in this sort of working atmosphere.

Not being noticed is particularly painful to someone who really pulls out all the stops and actually sees his efforts crowned with success, only to have his achievement ignored completely by everyone in the vicinity.

Does the following situation sound familiar to you? You have set yourself a difficult target to reach. You work hard for it. You

**56**

sail in a stormy sea, and everyone and everything seems to have plotted against you. Apart from this, it is all taking twice as long as planned. Sometimes you are very tempted to give up, but you force yourself to continue. In the end your persistence is rewarded. You are successful. The blood, sweat and tears were not in vain.

You have reached your goal. Grinning from one ear to the other you rush to tell your colleagues, friends and acquaintances about your great breakthrough – and their only reaction is stony silence.

Please do not make the mistake of assuming that you were not good enough, or that your success was not quite so important as you, in your innocence, had assumed. Those with the problem are the silent masses.

Many people have never attempted to make anything of their lives. Others had dreams which never became reality. They had bad experiences and gave up too soon. Perhaps a husband or wife made it difficult for them. Perhaps they hit upon a lousy boss who put paid to their job satisfaction. As a result they have come to a full-stop in their personal and professional development, and have had to come to terms with the fact that they do not stand a chance anymore. Their excuse: 'I am powerless. It's not my fault. All the paths are blocked.'

The inner equilibrium of such a person is destroyed when someone he compares himself with suddenly achieves something extraordinary. Self-doubt raises its head: 'Why he/she and not me? Perhaps I might have . . . if only . . .' The other's success awakens feelings of guilt: 'I shouldn't have given up so soon.' To protect the self, the realization of having failed has to be suppressed as much as possible. Thinking negatively about oneself causes anger, which expresses itself in aggression towards the successful person. Not reacting to something is also a form of punishment. A lack of response can be more destructive than a direct attack. A victim can defend himself against unjustified criticism; silence leaves him feeling disorientated. Is the achievement really so amazing? Is the other person too taken up with himself to pass feedback on to me? Is he trying to humiliate me by withholding recognition? At times of great defeats and great victories most people find themselves isolated.

A lack of feedback is the biggest killer of motivation at work. Nobody wants to be overlooked. The feeling that you have been passed over is a psychological burden which can cause various reactions. Some people develop an 'OK, take it easy' attitude, refusing to let themselves be put out. There is no point anyway. Others go into isolation: 'I can't get along with this person. I can't even bear to look at him. I don't want to have anything more to do with him.' Yet another group reacts aggressively, purposely ignoring norms and regulations: 'I'll make sure that they notice I'm here.'

A considerable number of conflicts stem from a permanent lack of attention. The results are an unwillingness to work hard, and low productivity. If, on the other hand, you take an interest in your staff, they will repay you with improved efficiency.

At the beginning of one seminar my client called me to one side with the following words of warning: 'There is one participant here who is a bit difficult. Jane Markham lived for 17 years abroad and is having some problems adjusting. She thinks she knows it all. She thought this seminar was beneath her because she worked as consultant herself and has nothing more to learn. I thought it better to let you know.'

I realized immediately that my only hope of winning Jane Markham over was to pay her the attention she was fighting so hard and so erroneously to gain at work.

The first question I asked at the beginning of the seminar was: 'Who has taken part in a seminar of this kind before?' Three participants raised their hands. Quite intentionally I looked at Jane Markham and said: 'We are a very big group. I should be most grateful if one of you could assist me in my role as course leader.' There was no doubt about it: Jane Markham wanted to.

She acted as group-leader, helped me with the preparation and actually led a short plenary session herself. Jane Markham blossomed and assured me several times that it was an excellent seminar and I was a superb course leader.

This was not manipulation on my part. I merely recognized that she was a dedicated person with a clear need to prove her abilities. All I did was to give her an opportunity to realize potential.

Showing an interest and passing on feedback are particularly important when engaging and training new staff. First impressions are decisive for people's real attitude towards the company. It is very dangerous to leave new staff stuck waiting in the wings.

I started my professional career at the age of 18 as a journalist on a daily paper. Instead of being sent out with experienced colleagues hunting for stories, or being introduced to the work of a reporter in some other way, for the first four weeks I was banished to the archives. It was my task to cut out newspaper articles. After a while I decided to take things into my own hands and started writing articles myself, all of which ended up in the waste-paper basket. My self-confidence fell to zero, and I developed a negative attitude towards my boss and colleagues. I did not do anything like my best, and handed in my notice as soon as my training period was completed.

It was cold comfort when I subsequently discovered that the

treatment I had experienced was not a reflection on me personally, but a kind of misguided testing probation which all new staff had to go through.

It does not take very long to break down someone's self-confidence, but it takes an awfully long time to build it up again.

To be condemned to passivity while other colleagues are groaning about the size of their workload is very demoralizing. New arrivals frequently ask themselves why they have been employed in the first place. Since they have no opportunity to contribute anything, they receive no feedback either. They feel disappointed and superfluous. All the hopes they had placed in the new post are unfulfilled. Motivation dissolves.

In companies where there is strong in-house competition, new colleagues are often consciously excluded. Withholding deserved recognition is one method of wielding power.

A person who is not very self-confident then feels rejected. He experiences the lack of feedback as an unspoken criticism: 'I suppose I'm not good enough.' Women in particular are in danger of falling into this trap. To earn their place they work from dawn to dusk and take work home with them. They bury themselves in specialist literature, and attend external in-service training courses. All this hard work has but one objective: to make their boss and their colleagues realize how hard-working, able and intelligent they are. But however much effort they make, this confirmation is not forthcoming.

It may happen that this particular lone warrior is lucky enough to have contact with clients. As she does everything possible to satisfy their requirements she receives from them the recognition so sadly missing in the workplace.

Such a situation can prove extremely confusing: outside the company masses of praise, inside not a single word. Why? The answer may well be because colleagues run her down to the manager, invent stories and manipulate the truth. In-house competition is pitiless. Help the new woman and risk someone else gaining from my hard-earned knowledge? No thank you! It is more advantageous to one's own career to make sure she is socially isolated.

A lack of response kills personal involvement. Some critics might claim that grown-up people should take responsibility for their own well-being. The keyword in this context is 'self-management'. One should not be dependent on others, but act as one thinks fit in a given situation. In principle, this is perfectly all right. Apparently, self-management is based on inner strength, but for a person who genuinely believes in himself it is unnecessary to keep his environment at a distance. On the contrary, it is probably precisely the person who has to over-compensate for a feeling of inner weakness who will choose to appear strong and independent by going it alone.

You are not born trusting in yourself, it is something you build up through cooperation and interaction with your environment. Positive experiences and good results are the building bricks. The American authors Morrison, White and Velsor have written in their book *Breaking the Glass Ceiling*,

> 'Direct experience, or success itself, is the most powerful source of confidence. It works like this: A manager succeeds at something and, as a result, becomes more confident and willing to take risks. The manager then takes on something that is more difficult and, with confidence, again succeeds. Success breeds confidence and risk taking, which, in turn, breed more success.'

In this context, the behaviour of the people in your immediate environment plays an important role. The extent to which you value yourself increases in a good working atmosphere, and is deadened by human coldness.

We are dependent on others as long as we live. It is an illusion to dream of complete and total independence, and believing in your own infallibility is nothing more than contempt for the rest of the human race. If everyone were to believe that they were so independent, that nobody else mattered at all, companies would become places where lone wolves fought it out amongst themselves for the rights of the strongest. In an atmosphere of this kind it is quite impossible to bring about synergy.

## A snapshot, not a work of art

Feedback means judging the attitudes, actions and achievements of others. What one person observes and feels is not the objective truth, but a subjective perception. Each person looks through the filter of his own values and experiences.

Feedback is a snapshot, taken here and now, which could look quite different just a moment later. A photograph taken of you at a business conference will show a completely different person from the one featured at home in the sitting room. In some people's presence you feel secure and at ease. They can confront you with unpleasant things without you getting angry. Others you prefer to keep at a distance and you treat them quite unlike your family or friends. The sort of picture people you keep at a distance have of you probably does not coincide with your own self-portrait in the least.

Thus your own behaviour can be seen to elicit specific reactions from other people. If you become aware of the kind of signals you transmit in a given situation you will be able to predict the way other people will react to you with a high degree of accuracy. You get as good as you give.

To illustrate this point I shall describe four types of behaviour using the example of four human caricatures: the misunderstood martyr, the aggressive bulldozer, the power-hungry manipulator, and the self-confident person. In reality, each of us has some of the characteristics of each of these types.

The misunderstood martyr is someone who complains a lot, and who is full of self-pity, but never actually does anything to improve the situation. His basic attitude is 'There's no point'. It is always somebody else's fault. Parents, husband, wife, boss or society in general are all or singly responsible for the miserable state of his existence. The misunderstood martyr wields power over others by making them feel guilty, but even when they do try to help him, what they do is quite irrelevant because it is never enough or it comes too late. After a while, given half a chance, people will avoid him like the plague. Naturally, this then confirms his paranoid conviction that the world is a dreadful place, and everyone is against him. The misunderstood martyr himself has simply not understood that he is responsible for his own life, and that it is his own moaning and groaning which make others keep their distance.

The aggressive bulldozer uses his elbows instead of convincing people. His philosophy of life is 'Those who do not love me shall fear me.' The staff do what the manager wants because they are scared of him. But fear kills off creativity. Many people do not dare to ask questions or to take an initiative. Taking risks is far too dangerous. What emerges is a disciplined flock of sheep who only react to orders from above. Staff punish an absolutist ruler by being uninterested and uninvolved in their work. They do what is required, but not that little bit extra that motivated staff do willingly. Those who are not so easily intimidated hit back openly. Conflict is the inevitable consequence. The aggressive bulldozer is not a good manager because he is unable to make use of his staff's resources. As a person he is nonetheless easier to get on with than the misunderstood martyr. His behaviour may be unpleasant, but at least it is transparent and predictable.

The power-hungry manipulator is an over-ambitious, egocentric person who would kill his own grandmother if it were to his own advantage. He builds up his position of power by licking the boots of his superiors, and taking on responsibility for ever more diverse fields until he holds all the reins in his hand. He achieves this by being helpful and pleasant to those above him while conspiring against his colleagues and those below him. By manipulating the truth a tiny bit he manages to sow the seed of doubt about other people's motives; by coming out with dubious hints and snide comments he breeds uncertainty around him. He is clever enough never to get his own hands dirty, but to let others do his dirty work. Thus it is impossible to pin him down with anything specific. In this kind of working environment it is dangerous to be open. Everyone is on their guard.

The power-hungry manipulator climbs up the first few rungs of the ladder very quickly but he rarely reaches the top. To keep everything under control he has to do everything himself. He is quite incapable of working in a team, and has made himself many enemies among those who feel he has trampled all over them. The higher he ascends in the hierarchy, the less able he is to maintain a superior level of knowledge in the various fields of his responsibility. During his steep climb he forgot to create a network of alliances on which he would now have to rely. He is in danger of making wrong decisions because he never listens to others, or because they fail to support him. In the long run, the power-hungry manipulator is anything but an efficient manager.

The responsible, self-confident person has realized that getting on means being able to give and take. Due to his well-balanced personality he is able to express his opinions openly and directly. He knows that it is sometimes necessary to formulate unpleasant things, but manages to make criticism constructive. He says 'What can we learn from it?' instead of 'Who was responsible for this mess?' He knows his own strengths and weaknesses, and is confident enough to praise other people's presentation. He brings out the best in everybody while taking care that individual results are never achieved at the cost of the company as a whole. His method of management involves constant dialogue with his staff in which they can discuss both positive and negative points without the least fear of recriminations.

No human being is as one-track as the types described above. Nevertheless, the aim should be to pursue self-development along the lines of the responsible, self-confident person, and this requires self-knowledge and training in communication skills and cooperation. Personal development should go hand in hand with developing the ability to work together successfully in a team.

Notwithstanding vigorous training in communication and cooperation techniques, people are susceptible to emotional vacillation. One and the same person may be very reserved one day and quite open the next.

Karin has decided to hand in her notice, but is waiting for confirmation of her new job from the firm where she has been for interview. In the lunch hour she chats to a colleague about this and that. Suddenly he asks her 'What do you hope to achieve in the next few years?' Karin is taken aback because she does not want to reveal her secret just yet. 'I'm not going to tell you that!' she blurts our, whereupon her astounded colleague remarks 'You're very reserved, aren't you?'

When the remark was made Karin felt misunderstood. But the longer she thought about it she tended to accept her colleague's feedback. At that particular moment she must have 'made a reserved impression' on him, although she always thought of herself as open and sociable, and certainly not as a 'reserved person'.

In this example, Karin wishes to prevent her colleague from finding out anything before she is quite certain that the new job is hers. Consequently, she does not want to pursue the topic. In another context, the colleague's question might well have been the catalyst for a discussion about the working atmosphere. She might have told him that poor cooperation with colleagues or the boss were gradually making her withdraw into herself. Perhaps he would even have been encouraged to draw conclusions about aspects of his own behaviour which might not have helped the situation.

The salient point with regard to feedback is not who is right, but that a dialogue gets underway which leads to a common understanding of reality.

Positive feedback is not always positive, and negative feedback is not always negative. What is decisive are the motives behind it and the way it is passed on.

# Positive feedback

In reply to the question 'How important is praise and recognition to you?', 92% of those completing my questionnaire registered +1 or +2. This result is of particular interest in relation to the question 'Do you think you are given the positive feedback you deserve and expect?' In this case, only 43% were satisfied (+1) or very satisfied (+2).

### Praise which pleases and encourages

For praise to please and encourage it has to be:

- genuine and honest
- specific
- face-to-face
- from the heart

**63** *Genuine and honest*  Praise must be genuine and honest. If people go around soft-soaping each other without really meaning what they say, praise soon degenerates into empty 'speechifying'.

*Specific*   Specific means that the praise articulated should refer to a particular matter, i.e. not be general or exaggerated. Generalizations like 'always' and 'never' are inevitably incorrect. Unspecified compliments such as 'The whole thing is absolutely A1!' give no indication as to what was really good and what could have been better.

The amount of praise should be proportionate to the service rendered or task carried out. Exaggerated recognition for the smallest of services arouses mistrust: 'Is he trying to flatter me? What does he hope to achieve?'

*Face-to-face*   On principle, people should be praised face-to-face. A manager should always take the trouble to speak to his staff directly, and not give the job of passing on praise to a third party.

*From the heart*   Recognition must come from the heart. As it is so very difficult to congratulate someone on something you would have liked to have had or done yourself, some people tend to mix a bitter pill in with their praise in the form of a condescending remark or sarcastic aside. Sometimes positive words come flowing out of their mouths while their eyes are aflame with jealousy and envy. Any pleasure is soon destroyed.

**Praise can be a form of contempt**

Pleasant words can act as a cover for contempt when the motive behind them is manipulation, or when they indicate that the expectations of the person giving the praise are too low. Women in particular often feel undervalued when their boss praises them for something they themselves take for granted while failing to comment on the achievements they are proud of.

I held my first seminar as a management consultant together with my boss. I was new in the company, and was still in the process of learning their methods. When the seminar came to an end I was absolutely exhausted, but fairly satisfied with my achievement. I asked my boss for feedback in the hope of benefiting from his experience. His only comment was: 'I was very impressed by your writing on the flipchart.'

What you expect from someone influences what they are prepared to achieve. High expectations prove you trust them and inspire them to work harder. Minimal expectations are a form of contempt, and have a demotivating effect.

A bank clerk published an article in a journal. Her boss saw it and offered the following praise: 'The article is very good. Did you write it yourself?'

Praise which includes devaluing elements is extremely annoying, because few people are able to counter it spontaneously. Later on, when you are lying awake in bed at night, you think of the most brilliant riposte. Your resentment at being undervalued by the other person is compounded by your anger with yourself for not having mastered the situation self-confidently. Instead of concentrating on your work your thoughts revolve around paying the other person back. Bitterness eats into your soul.

Women often complain about being paid the wrong sort of compliment in the wrong place. In their professional lives women are pleased to be praised for their working achievements, but they do not want to hear compliments about their hair or their clothes. These belong in the private sphere.

A female manager held a lecture on strategic planning. Afterwards, a colleague came up to her and commented admiringly: 'I didn't know that you had such beautiful legs, Anne!'

The motive for praising someone can also be manipulative. This category comprises all compliments which are geared to achieving advantages for the person making them. For example: flattering the boss in the hope of getting promotion, or the famous trick of upwardly delegating responsibility.

An employee says to the manager 'You are such a superb negotiator and know Mr Foster much better than I do. I think we could achieve much more if you were to be good enough to take on this particular case.' Reading between the lines, he is actually saying 'This is your baby, mate. I'm not going to risk burning my fingers on it.'

Manipulatory praise is very common in the home. A husband says to his wife 'You're a fantastic cook. I could never be as good as you are.' Roughly translated as 'Just you keep on doing all the cooking and spare me the trouble.'

Positive feedback is important, but it must be honest and not engendered by ulterior motives.

## Accepting positive feedback

Accepting positive feedback is an art.

- Never reject a compliment.
- Accept praise for what it is.
- Don't always look for the negative.
- Allow yourself to show your feelings.

*Never reject a compliment*   False modesty makes many people reject compliments: 'Oh, I do like your jumper'; 'What this old thing? I bought it years ago in the sales.'

The person who was trying to say something positive gets the feeling he has said something stupid, and thus made himself look ridiculous.

*Accept praise for what it is*   Others do not manage to accept praise for what it is. They would like to have a Jaguar, and are disappointed when they only get a Ford: 'I really admire you for being so articulate. Even at large-scale meetings you remain so cool when your turn comes to speak'; 'Well, that's nothing to get excited about.'

In this case the recipient of the praise was offended because he had expected more. He wanted to be flavour of the month, everybody's darling, and was not satisfied with just being praised for his rhetorical abilities.

*Don't always look for the negative*   Ambitious people demand a great deal of themselves, and often have a masochistic urge to be criticized for not being perfect. They only ever look for the negative, and ignore the positive. A lecturer has prepared his material thoroughly, and soon realizes intuitively that he has won his audience over. In the subsequent discussion, however, one troublemaker announces: 'That was a load of old rubbish.'

The lecturer is extremely hurt by the comment but he pulls himself together and answers diplomatically: 'I am speaking from personal experience which means a lot to me. Obviously I haven't managed to convince you. I'm sorry I haven't got anything better to offer you.'

The other participants are perfectly satisfied. Many flock around him after the lecture and want to know this or that. Nonetheless, the evening is ruined. The only words reverberating in his head are 'old rubbish'.

*Allow yourself to show your feelings*   Positive feedback can be overwhelming, especially when it comes unexpectedly. There is nothing disgraceful about showing your feelings.

I once took on a management-seminar lasting ten days. The organizer had booked a cheap and totally unsuitable hotel as a venue, and everything which could possibly go wrong did.

It started with all the participants arriving one day too early. It had been planned that everyone should arrive on the Tuesday evening after Easter so that we could begin the seminar on Wednesday morning. In the invitation sent out by the employer, however, reference to the arrival time had been left out, and the participants thought the seminar would begin on Tuesday morning. Many of them had cut short their Easter holidays, and others had got up at 4am in order to arrive punctually at 8.30 in the morning, only to find that the leader of the seminar did not turn up until well into the afternoon. The welcome I received was not exactly heart-felt!

The seminar room was far too small, the ceiling too low, and it soon became unbearably stuffy. There was no air-conditioning, and no point in opening the window because of the deafening noise of building works outside.

And on top of all, it was raining. The idea of lounges or informal places to sit had not actually occurred to the architect, and the only place you could flee to was a tiny, dark bar where all the other hotel guests also ended up. The cigarette smoke was stifling.

The course atmosphere was lousy. I tried everything I could think of to cheer the group up and encourage them to participate, but it was like trying to squeeze blood out of a stone. Nothing helped.

Gradually, I began to long for the moment when I could get rid of this miserable bunch. There is always interaction between the participants and the course leader. If the one side shows interest and participates actively, it inspires the other, and vice versa.

At an evaluation session on the evening of the fourth day the breakthrough eventually came. Quite unexpectedly one participant announced 'I thought it was really interesting today.' I could not believe my ears, but the next person continued 'I've learnt a lot. You are really very good.' And the third, 'Very professional, good presentation. The role play has helped me to gain some new insights.' And so it went on with everybody showering me with praise.

I was dumb-struck, and stared at the group in utter amazement. Were they mad or was I? Suddenly all the pent-up tension and frustration of the last few days broke and I started to bawl my head off. There sat the leader of the seminar in front of 20 seasoned businessmen crying her eyes out, eye-make up running down her face, unable to say a single word.

## Negative feedback

In reply to the question in my survey 'How important is it to you to receive constructive criticism?', 90% answered that it was important (+1) or even very important (+2).

In response to the question 'Are you given the negative feedback you expect and deserve?', only 40% answered 'yes'.

In theory, we all know that constructive criticism is just as important as praise. One employee noted, 'If everyone were brave enough to put constructive criticism into words, we could all get more enthusiastic about being praised, too. We would be sure that it was meant sincerely and really deserved.'

Yet in spite of knowing it in theory and being full of good intentions, many people shy away from expressing their dissatisfaction. Even in the framework of seminars, using exercise forms geared to breaking down inhibitions, many people try to avoid the issue: 'It's artificial', or 'We don't know each other well enough' and, as a last resort, 'I really can't think of anything.'

By contrast, the same people prove extremely animated when it comes to picking holes in someone behind their back. In private they pour their heart out; 'It's just awful.' They choose to unburden themselves on an innocent third party rather than confronting the person causing their problems directly. They are afraid of hurting others and ending up worse off than they were before.

A fear of hurting others is frequently unfounded. It is the choice of words which is decisive, i.e. the way in which criticism is presented. Negative feedback can be phrased so that its effect is encouraging: 'I am convinced you are capable of doing XYZ even better.'

Worrying about disadvantaging oneself is based on fear of retribution, or of making oneself unpopular. The latter is particularly a women's problem. From an early age they learn that it is their role to serve and sacrifice themselves for others. Their reward is love. Saying something negative straight out to somebody is the equivalent of failing in the essential role of caring for others. They fear, as a consequence, that they will not be loved.

A fear of being deprived of love is always lurking in the background. If a woman's work is criticized she often feels rejected on a personal level: 'I'm not good enough. No-one here likes me.' It is but a short step from here to self-pity: 'Haven't I made sacrifices? And this is all the thanks I get.' An over-developed need for recognition and acceptance can become an obstacle to the development of women's careers.

Just think for a moment about the differences between destructive and constructive criticism. When employees only ever get to hear what they are doing wrong, and not what they are doing well, the result is diminished motivation. A lower-grade civil service employee explained it as follows: 'Our superiors take it absolutely for granted that we do good work. But the tiniest error is turned into a major catastrophe.'

Another employee added 'It is especially frustrating when you have made a special effort to get something finished on time and then you are confronted with the boss's grim face or, even worse, total lack of interest.'

Negative attitudes are contagious. If one person is always grumbling it is not long before everyone develops a negative basic attitude both to the job and to other people at work. Ironic comments and jokes at other people's expense are frequently unconscious strategies for smoothing over a conflict brewing beneath the surface.

## Devastated by unfair criticism

During my seminars I often ask participants to talk about the way they react to unfair criticism.

Before reading any further, please take a sheet of paper and write down how you react to unfair criticism. When was the last time you felt annoyed by criticism? Who said what, and on which occasion? Why did you feel hurt? Compare your own answers with those in exercise 9.

## Constructive criticism

Constructive criticism can be very helpful. Here are a few suggestions for criticizing without hurting:

- Recognize good intentions.
- Be sure of your own motives.
- Say what you really want.
- Be concrete, spontaneous and direct.
- Choose the right moment.
- Accept that feedback is a two-way process.
- Say what your criticism is supposed to achieve.
- Confirm when a change has taken place.
- Threaten consequences.
- Put your threat into practice.

*Recognize good intentions* Not many people actually do the wrong thing intentionally. Even when they make a total mess of something, it was usually well-meant. Thus make the effort to recognize good intentions: 'I know that you have invested a lot of work in this report, but you might go into greater depth in paragraph xyz. This will clarify the argument overall.'

The clever superior builds up his staff's self-confidence. If, for example, he combines the negative elements with positive ones by referring to previous attainments, he indicates that he believes in someone's ability to do better. This is encouraging. The person being criticized can retain his self-respect, 'OK, I made a mistake, but I'm still a valuable human being.'

*Be sure of your own motives*  Before you open your mouth to give vent to your anger, be sure of your own motives: 'Why do I feel such a burning desire to be critical? What do I want to achieve with my criticism?' The only legitimate grounds for criticism are the wish to improve achievements or change attitudes and behaviour.

But if I am really honest with myself, I have to admit that I sometimes criticize because I am having a bad day. Someone has annoyed me, and now I need an outlet for letting off steam. Ignoble motives for criticizing include envy, jealousy, an inferiority complex, transferring earlier experiences to a new situation, and projecting one's own ill-humour onto others. These are usually unconscious processes which influence the way we act.

There is a Norwegian proverb which claims 'Envy is stronger than the sexual urge.' It requires strength to be genuinely pleased about other people's successes, and only self-confident people manage. But hardly anybody can be self-confident all the time, and in every situation. This is fertile ground for the growth of envy.

Shortly after founding my own company, INCITA Management, while I was still trying to discover my identity among the legions of management consultants, I worked on a seminar together with a colleague who, on the professional side, complemented me very well indeed.

My partner was extremely popular. She had great charisma, and her dedication enabled her to get the very best out of the participants. I was pleased about her success. But at the same time I was plagued by envy, feeling that she had pushed me into the background.

One day we divided the participants into two groups. She worked on her topics, I on mine. It happened that she overran the agreed timetable by half an hour, while I finished on time. My group had to wait for hers.

Suddenly I felt extremely angry. I managed to pull myself together until the official programme had come to an end. When we were alone I burst out, 'You must keep to the agreed timetable. I can't put up with you always running over the time. For goodness' sake be a bit more considerate.'

My anger was genuine, but the cause had very little to do with her poor time-keeping. The intensity of my emotional outburst was quite inconsistent with the error she had made. I was livid because I was jealous of her.

**70**  Once I had become aware of my own motives I gained the strength to stop criticizing her. I learned to value our cooperation, and to applaud her success. When she overran the agreed time on a subsequent occasion I managed to ask her in a friendly, quiet manner to keep to the arrangement we had made.

Envy and jealousy are human reactions. The more insecure we are, the greater the threat appears. The first step towards overcoming such 'hateful' feelings is to admit their existence to oneself. Only then can you start working on coming to terms with them. Suppression is worse than useless. This does not, however, mean that we can allow envy and jealousy free rein. Always consider what is most effective in the long run. An uncontrolled emotional outburst can destroy a relationship with another person completely. If you are able to recognize and accept your own weaknesses you will be in a stronger position to push aside niggling negative thoughts and destructive tendencies. You can work off your anger on paper. Write down everything that is troubling you, but never actually send a letter written in anger.

Inferiority complexes can cause similar reactions to envy. At one seminar the participants were supposed to pass on feedback to one another. A man said to a woman 'You're arrogant.' I asked him to explain why he found her arrogant. He answered honestly, 'I feel inferior because she is so articulate and I hardly dare open my mouth when there are a lot of people listening.'

Psychologists call this mode of behaviour 'projection'. It indicates people who loathe their own weaknesses to such a degree that they try to fight and punish them vicariously in other people. They transfer their dissatisfaction with themselves to others. Criticizing someone is thus a form of punishing them for having the same weakness, or for having strengths not possessed but desired by the person criticizing. The standard generation conflict, 'When I was your age that sort of thing didn't exist', or 'In my day . . .' can be understood in this light.

In *The Undiscovered Self*, C.G. Jung writes:

> 'The evil that comes to light in man and that undoubtedly dwells within him is of gigantic proportions . . . He does not deny that terrible things have happened and still go on happening, but it is always (others) who do them . . . This strengthens the opponent's position in the most effective way, because the projection carries the fear which we involuntarily and secretly feel for our own evil over to the other side and considerably increases the formidableness of this threat.'

In the language of psychology the word 'transfer' means that a person carries over feelings and opinions from previously experienced situations to the here and now. If a woman had a strict father who was mean with money, her husband can also expect at some stage to be accused of being strict and mean. If the previous manager was authoritarian, for some considerable time the staff will behave towards the new manager as though he were also standing there with a whip in his hand.

Those belonging to minority groups are frequently victims of stereotypes and generalizations. If an English person meets a Pole he tends to assume that he is going to be just like the Polish neighbour he lived next door to five years ago.

A Swedish woman worked for a manager who was married to a Swiss. He quite naturally assumed that she shared any number of opinions with his wife. After all, she was a woman, too, and a foreigner.

Being a management consultant means moving in a man's world, and many male managers assume female consultants are all the same. I particularly remember a sales discussion during which it was totally impossible for me to convince my client because the director kept on seeing in me another female consultant he had engaged years before, and whose methods he had not liked.

To get out of this transfer-trap you have to realize that there are very marked individual differences in any group of people: Swedes, Swiss, Poles, or indeed management consultants. Do not draw any hasty conclusions. Take the trouble to discover people anew.

Many conflicts derive from a lack of differentiation on the part of the person criticizing between previous experiences and the current situation.

*Say what you really want*   Say what you really want, but say it directly and fairly. If you are annoyed about something it is tempting to resort to the following destructive modes of behaviour:

- niggling
- generalizing
- attacking
- making someone look ridiculous.

These are certainly methods of letting off steam, but they create enemies – perhaps for all time. Nobody likes to be criticized. At the time it may be a great relief to see the other person writhing on the ground, but it can be assumed that he will eventually rise from the dust: how sweet is revenge.

Instead of delighting in others' errors you can take responsibility for your own well-being by saying 'I want/would like you to . . .' If you find it embarrassing to discuss certain matters, describe your feelings in words: 'I find it rather embarrassing . . .', or 'I'd really prefer not to mention it but . . .' If you give the other person an insight into how you are feeling deep down they will understand that you mean it seriously. Apart from this, it also helps to combat your own nervousness. Have a look at exercise 2.

The I-form is the most suitable for expressing negative criticism. In other situations the you-form may be more fitting. If I want to sell you something or convince you about my ideas I achieve better results if I tell you what advantages 'you' will gain from my offer rather than why 'I' would like to sell it. When passing on negative feedback, however, I can lessen the recipient's unease by giving expression to my own wishes and feelings, rather than confronting the other person with their incompetence.

*Be concrete, spontaneous and direct*   Pass on feedback immediately; do not wait until a minor problem has developed into a major catastrophe. Be concrete, and say exactly what disturbs you. Keep to the point and, when criticizing behaviour, avoid generalizations or personal attacks.

It is best to pass on negative feedback in private. If a whole department is affected by a problem it can be salutary to discuss what has gone wrong openly. But the pre-condition for this is a working atmosphere in which open discussion of controversial issues is generally accepted practice. What must be avoided at all costs is making a scapegoat of one individual in front of all the others.

Aggression frequently expresses itself indirectly in the form of hidden allusions, barbed remarks and jokes, against which the victim is unable to defend himself. Put yourself in the other person's position. Would you like to be made into a laughing stock? If you are genuinely interested in good communication, take your courage in both hands and address the person concerned directly. Do not grumble about him behind his back.

Give the person being criticized an opportunity to respond to the points you raise. Gossip and scandal-mongering only cause insecurity. The victim has the feeling that something is wrong, but does not know exactly what, and wastes masses of time and energy speculating who might have said what to whom.

A salesperson notes the following about the working atmosphere in his company:

'I once had an argument with a colleague and he has never forgiven me for it. He never speaks to me himself, but pulls the strings behind my back. I have the feeling that people gossip about me in secret, but I can't defend myself because I don't know exactly what's going on. I can't pin anything down, but I always have to be on my guard not to say the wrong thing. I hardly dare to open my mouth or react spontaneously.

One day I went into the canteen and the head of personnel was sitting there. I said hello and he smiled back. We've always got on well with each other. Then this colleague came along and sat down next to the personnel manager. They started talking to each other and when I left the room his manner was icy: not a word, not a smile. Now, was that just coincidence or had my colleague been getting at me again?'

Had this colleague really been plotting against the salesman, or was it just his imagination? He will never know the answer. The lack of direct communication has brought on a paranoid state. He has to be desperately careful because he thinks he is surrounded by enemies.

A year later the salesman was offered six months salary if he took 'voluntary' redundancy. The firm was unable to cite any professional failures, and thus had no formal grounds for firing him. The employee had simply become a burden on his environment because he felt persecuted, and thought everyone was conspiring against him. The lack of communication on this sensitive issue had negative consequences in both economic and psychological terms. The company had unnecessary expenditure to pay-off a well-qualified employee. The salesman suffered due to serious psychological pressure, and had difficulty in finding another job as potential new employers naturally checked his references. This could all have been avoided if the parties concerned had managed to talk to one another before the problems came to a head.

*Choose the right moment*   Even when criticism is fully justified, it is possible to select the wrong time for making it. An employee who has made a serious mistake is fully aware that something has gone wrong. He may be reproaching himself and losing sleep over the matter. In this situation his psychological state is so insecure that criticism might very well drive him into the depths of depression.

Choose the right moment for passing on your feedback. If you are in doubt, say 'I should like to speak to you about this matter. Would you like to talk about it straight away, or would you rather wait until tomorrow?'

*Accept that feedback is a two-way process*   If you have to take a member of staff to task, be prepared to be told to what extent your own behaviour has contributed to his or her lack of success. Feedback is a two-way process; especially when dealing with conflicts, it is essential that everyone concerned has a chance to speak.

*Say what your criticism is supposed to achieve*   Do not be satisfied with simply listing faults, but say what your criticism is supposed to achieve. As a manager it is your task to formulate objectives clearly and intelligibly. Many errors and conflicts stem from imprecise statements of objective. The employee does not know what exactly is expected of him.

*Confirm when a change has taken place*   If a member of staff changes his behaviour as a result of your ciriticism or achieves better results, be sure to make it clear to him that you realize what has happened. Do not be mean with recognition.

*Threaten consequences*   If the member of staff is totally deaf to your criticism and fails to make any attempt to adapt his behaviour, you have to transfer the conflict to a higher level and threaten consequences. Your threat should, however, be concomitant with the gravity of the situation. If, in the heat of battle, you allow yourself to make threats of extreme punishment which, on consideration, you would not dare to carry out, you merely begin to undermine your own authority. Your threats are empty; you lose your credibility.

### Accepting criticism

Accepting criticism is an art that very few people master. Most people try to avoid confrontation by denying what has been said, defending themselves, counter-attacking, or trying to find a scapegoat.

This negative attitude to criticism is a sign of insecurity. A confident person knows and accepts his strengths and weaknesses. An insecure person tries to cover up his weak points.

It is a shock to many to discover that other people see them quite differently from the way they see themselves. This is not least the case with managers who frequently have little contact with their staff. To avoid unpleasant situations they bury themselves in their work, are constantly sitting in meetings, cars or aeroplanes, or are generally otherwise engaged. The dark pin-striped suit, the enormous desk and the portrait gallery on the wall are all power symbols creating distance.

A manager had little contact with his staff, and did not know what they were thinking. Once an employee dared to make a suggestion he did not like. The manager was livid and 'punished' the employee with condescending remarks.

This was not a clever reaction. Although he did not share the employee's view, he could have used the opportunity to explain why he did this or that. In this way he would have avoided subsequent misunderstandings. Instead of explaining, he made the employee feel stupid. It is far better for differences of opinion to be aired openly than to have clusters of people whispering and speculating in dark corners.

If no-one has ever criticized you it probably means that you have never achieved anything significant.

**75**

Fear of criticism has its roots in childhood. The little boy and the little girl soon learn that they will be punished if they do something wrong: 'If you don't behave I won't let you go out/you won't be able to watch children's television/the bogey-man will come' or, even worse, 'If you don't do what Mummy says she won't love you any more.' Although the child is still too young to understand why something is wrong or forbidden, it becomes afraid and nervous, and feels guilty when it has made a mistake.

A child who constantly observes that criticism and punishment go together is influenced by this as an adult. But the spontaneous fear accompanying criticism is not there from birth; it is a product of education. As such, it is possible to unlearn this mode of behaviour by using methods and techniques which strengthen self-confidence.

A self-confident way of accepting criticism comprises:

- Accepting criticism without interrupting.
- Differentiating between impersonal and personal criticism.
- Listening closely to what is actually said, and not speculating what could conceivably be meant.
- Asking for clarification.
- Differentiating between justified, partially-justified and unjustified criticism.
- Admitting mistakes.
- Asking questions.
- Promising improvement.

*Listen without interrupting*   Listening quietly without immediately interrupting by trying to make explanations or excuses is a precondition for differentiating between justified and unjustified criticism. Even if the criticism appears unjust at the time, it may be that there is a grain of truth in there somewhere.

If you interrupt the person criticising you, you protect yourself from hearing something unpleasant, but you also rob yourself of the opportunity of learning something about yourself, and thus furthering your personal development.

*Differentiate between impersonal and personal criticism*   Many people are unable to differentiate between the person and the thing. They take every criticism to heart, and immediately consider themselves a failure or an innocent victim. Your reproachful, offended facial expression makes it difficult for the other person to present the criticism directly and precisely. He would rather beat about the bush and restrict himself to tentative implications. All this means is that the unsatisfactory situation remains unchanged, and the person being criticized learns nothing from his mistakes.

Whether criticism is painful or not depends to a large extent on the way it is presented, but also on the way the person being criticized views himself. Not to put too fine a point on it: no-one can manipulate another person against his will. People can only hurt you when their judgement falls on willing ears and confirms your own doubts.

A self-confident person, or someone in a familiar situation, is better able to deal with criticism than an insecure person, or someone in a new or unfamiliar situation.

A lack of self-confidence, and the concomitant inability to cope with criticism, are closely related to our early experiences. If, as a child or young person, someone constantly feels rejected, and their first experiences at work do nothing to build up their self-confidence, this can easily lead to a situation in which they believe that people are secretly plotting against them, and that nothing but evil can be expected from others. The mistrust that such a person displays and observes all around him releases in others the very reactions he fears and expects.

The threatening monster is a product of his own phantasy. This web of connections is well illustrated by the following caricature:

A woman is lying in bed having a terrible nightmare. An enormous gorilla climbs in through the window striking a threatening pose:

- 'What do you want?' the frightened woman cries.
- 'How should I know?' answers the gorrilla quietly, 'it's your dream.'

However, it is one thing to understand on the abstract level how one's picture of oneself influences emotional reactions, but quite another to break away from the habitual patterns of thought and behaviour.

Reason says that criticism can be both necessary and salutary. Criticism is nothing to be ashamed of; nobody is perfect. On top of this, not all criticism is justified. Some people only criticize because they do not like themselves. Others always look on the black side, and have lost the ability to recognize the positive elements in life. Apart from this, people are different and, as everyone knows, you cannot argue about taste. We all have different needs, ethical values and interests. It would be a miracle if we could all agree. Whatever any one person decides, there will always be others who are unhappy about it. Why make life difficult for yourself?

Unfortunately, the emotions see the matter quite differently. Up pops the small child out of the subconscious, waiting to be punished because it has not fulfilled others' expectations. Easily mobilized guilt feelings have a field-day. The age-old feeling of helplessness gains the upper hand and creates internal blocks.

Paradoxically, a bad conscience can trouble you even when you have not done anything wrong, but merely failed to do something you assume others had expected of you.

Unfounded feelings of guilt are more common in women than in men. Mothers still frequently expect their daughters to help in the house while their sons are allowed to continue playing. In traditional child-rearing, little girls are soon expected to accept responsibility for everyone and everything, while little boys are supposed to practise being heroes; rough and inconsiderate behaviour is almost *de rigueur*.

Even as adults, many women continue to feel responsible for others. Wives cosset their husbands by trying to predict their wishes and suppressing their own.

A family lived in a modest house. The children were gradually growing up. For years the mother had been looking forward to having her own room once the children were out of the house. When the time came the husband made the room into a den for himself. She was extremely disappointed, shed tears in private, and complained to her neighbour how egoistic her husband was. But the point was that she had never told her husband that she would have liked to have had the room for herself.

At the same time, she complained that her husband was useless in the house. By constantly sacrificing herself for the family she had prevented him from taking on more responsibility.

Working women often experience feelings of guilt about not having enough time for their children while they are at work, and not devoting enough of their energies to their job while they are home.

A permanently bad conscience leads to a situation in which ordinary impersonal criticism and totally neutral questions are seen as a personal attack. The manager might ask 'Have you finished your work?', or 'How far did you get?.' The employee's heart sinks, and he starts accusing himself: of course, he could have finished ages ago if . . . He now feels unjustly criticized, and reacts with a counter-attack: 'You know how much I've got to do . . . And apart from that, you could have given me the stuff earlier, then I'd have . . . And you could divide the work up a bit more fairly. John Smith sits twiddling his thumbs all day while I'm absolutely drowning in work. I could do with rather more consideration from you.'

**78** Thus the manager asks a perfectly harmless question. The employee thinks he is being criticized, and reacts with a mixture of self-pity and aggression.

The only way to free yourself of unfounded guilt feelings is to get to know yourself better, and to recognize, accept and work on your weak points. Exercise 14 should prove helpful.

Listen closely to what the other person is saying, and do not speculate what he might conceivably mean. You often only hear what you want or expect to hear.

I once took part in a seminar on self-management. It was a cold December day, and the room was poorly heated. In the middle of the lecture I had to go out and fetch my coat from the cloakroom. Once I was outside it suddenly occurred to me that I really ought to make a few telephone calls.

Quarter of an hour later I returned to the lecture. Just as I opened the door I heard the leader of the seminar say, 'This is quite intolerable!' I immediately assumed this comment referred to me. Luckily, I managed to pull myself together and asked, 'Could you repeat what you just said? What did you mean "This is quite intolerable!"?' The leader answered, 'That the room's so poorly heated. I'm going to complain to the management.'

When there are disagreements and conflicts of interest, those concerned often try quite consciously to accuse each other of dishonourable opinions and attitudes. They twist each other's words around. Political debates offer a wealth of examples. The recipe for manipulation is: first make a false claim about what the opponent has said, meant or intended. Then start to attack this claim to emphasize one's own integrity. If the opponent falls into the trap he will also try to counter-attack, i.e. he will start defending the claim made in his name, and hence points of view he does not actually hold.

If people really want to misunderstand each other because this serves their own purposes, no techniques for improving communication in the world can be of any help. If, on the other hand, you are genuinely interested in the other person's opinion, but are not quite sure whether you have understood him properly, then you should ask for clarification.

*Ask for clarification* It is a sign of strength to ask for more information about something unpleasant. Ask open questions which cannot be simply be answered with 'yes' or 'no':

- 'Could you explain that more fully, please?'
- 'Please tell me precisely what it is that you are not happy about.'
- 'How would you yourself have done it? What would you yourself recommend?'

- 'What would you like me to do? What is it you expect me to do?'

In this way, the other person is forced to re-think and clarify his claims. If the criticism is justified he will be able to present convincing arguments. If he is only using you as an outlet for his anger, he will probably not be able to come up with an answer:

Participant: 'I didn't like the exercise we did yesterday.'
Course leader: 'Could you explain that more fully, please? What exactly didn't you like?'
Participant: 'I felt as though I'd been forced into something against my will . . . You should have asked us about doing things like that first.'

In this case the criticism appears to be justified. The course leader had apparently chosen an unsuitable exercise, or an unsuitable moment for doing a particular exercise. This feedback helps him to judge the situation better in future:

Headhunter: 'What was your relationship to your previous boss?'
Applicant: 'In the company I used to work for I often felt there was an enormous gap between company theory and practice. The ethical values propagated by my boss in his official speeches bore no relation whatsoever to his own behaviour.'
Headhunter: 'One could say the same about you.'
Applicant: 'What do you mean? Could you explain to what you are referring?'
Headhunter: 'It's rather difficult to say, really.'

In this real-life example, the headhunter was trying to provoke the applicant to see how he reacted in stress situations. The applicant was very surprised by the insinuation which was obviously pure invention. By asking for clarification he gained time to think; when the headhunter was unable to substantiate his claims, the applicant knew what he had been aiming at.

*Differentiate between justified, partially-justified and unjustified criticism*   Listen carefully, and try to discover whether the criticism is justified, partially-justified, or totally unjustified.

### *Justified criticism*
Justified criticism is feedback on a mode of behaviour which you can and should change, or a standard of work which you can and should improve. The ability to accept criticism is an important factor in being successful, and vice versa. Someone who is incapable of admitting that he has made a mistake risks coming to a full-stop in his career, notwithstanding his professional capabilities.

In *Breaking the Glass Ceiling*, Morrison, White and Velsor write:

> 'Some senior executives regarded taking advice and criticism as a strong, positive factor in the struggle of women to adapt to the workplace. Listening to feedback was a success factor cited for 7 of the 19 successful women described by savvy insiders: she had a tendency to get visibly upset if something was happening that she didn't like, and also to be very defensive. I spoke to her about the first problem, and she changed. One of her great assets is the ability to listen and make changes.'

Be prepared to own up to your mistakes.

- 'Yes, it's true, I did . . .'
- 'Yes, you're right.'

Contribute yourself to clearing the matter up by encouraging the other person to get his anger off his chest. If you do not get it sorted out straight away he may well hold it against you for years. Thus ask open questions:

- 'What are the problems I have caused you?'
- 'Is there anything else you would like to talk to me about?'
- 'How do you feel about things now?'

Be grateful for feedback:

- 'I am very grateful that you . . .'
- 'Thank you for the feedback. I've learned a lot from it.'

Say what you intend to do in order to solve the problem:

- 'I'll look into the matter again and I'll certainly get it finished by . . .'
- 'I'll think about it all very carefully.'

### Unjustified criticism

Criticism is unjustified when you are not responsible for the mistake, or when the true motives are not those officially stated. Unjustified criticism is objectively incorrect or exaggerated. The sole aim is to affect the person being criticized by hurting him, offending him, humiliating him, manipulating him, or making him look ridiculous.

What is the best way of defending oneself against such treatment? Stone-age man sitting in his cave and seeing an enormous bear outside only had one alternative: attack or run for his life. In situations of physical danger modern man also feels instinctively whether it is better to fight or run. To meet psychological challenges, however, it is possible to adopt verbal techniques which allow you to choose a third option, and to indicate to the aggressor, quite self-confidently, just how far he can go.

Unjustified criticism is often made by insecure people who wish to emphasize their own excellence through humiliating others. Those active in academic circles are particularly pitiless. Nobody should get the impression that one is 'uncritical', i.e. naive and ignorant. If someone is lecturing about polar bears on Spitzbergen he may end up being criticized because what he has said is not relevant to camels in the Sahara.

When you're lecturing and are asked questions which have nothing to do with the topic in hand, or are presented with contrary opinions which you are sure have been worked out at home in advance long before anyone had heard what you had to say, you can always ask 'What is your opinion on the matter?', or 'What solution would you suggest?'

Now your suspicion may well be confirmed that the person concerned was not in the least interested in hearing an answer to the question asked, but merely wished to place himself in the limelight. Thank him by saying 'That was an excellent answer to your question.'

Querulous, niggling people often lack self-confidence, and have an inordinate need for confirmation. Be generous and grant your adversary the recognition he is so desperately trying to find. It is one way of turning some enemies into friends.

Allow your adversary to make his opinion known, whether or not you happen to be of the same opinion yourself: 'I know that you think . . .' This does not of course mean 'I fully share your opinion', but simply confirms that you have registered the other person's point of view.

Now you are in a position to decide whether you want to throw the argument open – 'That's totally wrong!' – and embark on full-scale conflict, or whether the issue is so unimportant and the time so unsuitable that you prefer not to waste your energies on a war of words. If the latter is the case, it is amazing what can be achieved by letting your opponent stick to his own opinion. It sounds paradoxical, but if you try it, you will find that it is an excellent way of taking the wind out of someone's sails.

Agree with someone when they are right:

Criticism: 'Now you are not being consistent.'
Answer: 'No, you're right, I'm not. In relation to what I said at the time I'm being inconsistent. But I've thought about it very carefully and, apart from that, since then I've received some more up-to-date information, so now I'm actually in favour of a different strategy.'

Give your adversary to understand that, in theory, he could be right.

An otherwise punctual and conscientious employee once turned up a few minutes late for work. His pedantic boss was standing in the door, looking at his watch: 'I suppose you realize that we start work here at 8 o'clock', he rebuked him.

Reply: 'Yes, you're right. I am a bit late today. I quite agree with you that it would be a major problem if everyone always arrived hours late.'

In this case, the employee admits his error ('a bit late'), and enlarges the scope of the problem ('everyone', 'always', 'hours late'). Thus, in theory, he agrees that his boss is right.

Be prepared to allow for situations in which your adversary might be right:

Criticism: 'You seem to have let everything get out of control.'
Answer: 'You're quite right. I am very, very busy, and there are days when I can barely keep up with my own pace of work.'

In other circumstances you might accept the criticism, if the error had been more serious, for example, or if it had happened frequently or in a different situation.

If you do not wish to let your adversary think he is right on any account, you can remove the barbs anyway simply by repeating what he has said himself:

Criticism: 'I wouldn't wear a mini-skirt if I were your age.'
Answer: 'This skirt is rather short, isn't it?'

You have got the message. There is nothing more to be said because you are not going to let yourself be provoked.

The American psychologist Manuel J. Smith calls this technique 'fogging'. In his book *When I Say No, I Feel Guilty*, he uses the following metaphor:

'If you throw a stone at a thick wall of fog you cannot see where it lands. Unlike hitting the wall of a house it does not ricochet. If you do not meet with resistance there is no fun in throwing more stones. If you are the recipient of unjustified criticism you can spoil your critic's fun by clothing your own opinions, reactions and feelings in fog. You thus become unassailable.'

In this context I should like to emphasize that fogging is most helpful in tackling unjustified criticism aimed at debasing or manipulating someone. Justified criticism needs to be answered. In many companies, motivation and productivity would grow considerably if the management were more open to the critical opinions held by their staff.

**83**

*Partially-justified criticism*

Partially-justified criticism contains a grain of truth, but only a grain. It turns a peccadillo into a great fault (exaggeration), or generalizes about a one-off event (generalization).

Accept those elements of the criticism which are justified, and reject those which are unjustified:

Manager: 'You're never at your desk when I need you.'

Employee: 'You're right. At 3 o'clock (specification) I was at a meeting about . . . But it really isn't true that I'm never there (rejecting unjustified criticism). I should be grateful if you would let me know if you are going to need me for something urgent (I-form).'

Criticism: 'You'll never get it right.'

Answer: 'I realize that you had had different ideas about this (you are right). Please tell me exactly how you would like this report to be prepared (asking for clarification). I really would like you to be satisfied with my work (I-form and rejecting the criticism).'

Woman: 'You only ever think of yourself and never help me with the washing-up.'

Man: 'It's true (you are right) that I didn't wash-up immediately after dinner tonight (specification). I was feeling exhausted after work. But you're being unfair if you say I never help (rejecting criticism if it really is unjustified!). What difference does it make if I leave it until later, or even until tomorrow morning? (asking for clarification).'

# 7 | The art of listening

Open communication assumes that the person sending the message expresses him- or herself clearly and accurately, and that the recipient is prepared to listen. Listening shows respect.

But most people are bad listeners. Some of the typical barriers to communication are:

- Too much information in one go.
- Lack of confidence.
- Preparing what you are going to say yourself.
- Selective listening.

## Too much information in one go

The amount of information a person can absorb is very restricted. If we are presented with too much all at once we simply switch off.

Someone who gushes forth information is wasting his time and energy because the listener will only absorb a small percentage of his outpourings. If you speak excitedly or nervously and heap one argument on top of the other, the effect will be correspondingly reduced. If you wish to convince other people about something, you are well advised to take a few deep breaths and then divide up your grandiose ideas into small portions.

## Lack of confidence

85 | People who feel insecure are often bad listeners. Imagine an

official reception where you hardly know anybody, but have to carry out representative duties, or the opening of a seminar. Now, be honest, how many names can you remember after the first round of introductions? Most people are far too taken up with preparing their own contribution to listen to the others. Thus it is important to create a relaxed atmosphere at a seminar before the participants start introducing themselves to one another.

Research carried out by the American communications expert Albert Mehrabian has revealed that, when we meet someone for the first time, we concentrate 55% on body language, 38% on voice, and only 7% on what the person actually says. When you are dreading the next reception, just remember that what you say is of much less significance than the signals transmitted by your body language. Smile, ask questions and listen. This is one way of gaining someone's sympathy without having to hold forth at length yourself.

## Preparing what you are going to say yourself

In our competitive society, discussions can soon turn into bitter fights about who is right and who is wrong. The more articulate person is likely to win the war of words even if his solution is not necessarily the better one.

When people are arguing with each other over differences of opinion they are frequently at odds because the one is preparing what he is going to say while the other one is speaking. To avoid misunderstandings it is essential to listen to what the other person is saying before leaping in with your own objections.

Television debates between politicians from opposing parties are a frightening example of this. The politicians do not even try to answer the interviewer's questions, but just reel off what they have prepared in advance. When discussing points with their opponents they do not listen either, but fire their own cannon, twist the other person's words, imply he has meant things he has not actually said, and refer to supposed previous remarks which can no longer be verified because they were made such a long time ago that no-one can remember precisely how they were phrased. Tactical manoeuvres of this kind may be necessary for surviving in politics, but in business they will not get you very far. The best salesman is the one who lets his customers do all the talking and takes their problems seriously.

## Selective listening

**86** The ability to listen is also related to one's own expectations. A person listens when he thinks that what is said is interesting, important and useful. He often imagines that he knows what is going to be said in a given situation, and does not bother to listen at all.

If someone has no great expectations in a relationship he will not take very much notice of the other person. A woman says something during a discussion. No-one reacts to any extent. A little while later a man takes up her idea and develops it further. Everyone now turns their attention to him. And in minutes his name is recorded as the originator of the idea. Even today it is quite common for both men and women not to have high expectations of other women. What a woman says cannot be that important.

However, the same phenomenon can also be observed in all-female groups. The most well-known woman or the one with the highest position receives the most attention, even when she is only repeating what someone has said before her.

Status-bound modes of behaviour of this kind are linked with the internal attitude towards authority. Many want to bathe in other people's glory. They want to gain power by being close to those in power, and so they grant the most attention to the person with the highest status.

People also tend to listen selectively during arguments, or when they feel provoked. A lecturer says something which annoys someone in the audience. It may well have been something quite peripheral, totally unrelated to the main topic of the lecture. But whatever the lecturer now goes on to say, the person concerned will no longer listen, but get more and more excited, considering how he can get his own back on the lecturer afterwards.

Most people think they are good listeners. Test yourself by turning to exercise 4.

# 8 | How to ask questions

It is better to ask some of the questions than to know all of the answers.

*James Thurber*

To know how to talk to people means, among other things, knowing how to ask the right questions. Asking questions shows that you are involving yourself and interested in other people.

Begin a conversation with questions:

- What?
- Who?
- How?
- Which?
- When?

Avoid why-questions. The innocent little word 'why' frequently implies a hidden accusation: 'Why are you late?' ('What have you been up to? I don't trust you!').

The following examples are inspired by the book *Smart Questions for Successful Managers* by Dorothy Leeds.

## Negotiations

Show that you are prepared to be flexible by asking your negotiating partner 'Which topic do you think we should deal with first?'

## Job interviews

One of the favourite questions in job interviews is 'Tell us something about yourself.'

Applicants often make the mistake of wasting valuable time by starting with Adam and Eve instead of getting straight down to points that are relevant to the new job. Instead of losing themselves in childhood memories, applicants can ask 'What would you like to know? What are you particularly interested in?'

## Telephoning

You are trying to ring an important person, but either the secretary refuses to put you through or the person himself is constantly away. Instead of telling off the secretary, who is only following her boss's instructions, you can ask politely: 'Could you tell me when would be the best time to reach Mr Brown, and how? This is really very important to me. You'd be doing me an enormous favour.'

## The working atmosphere

During a meeting your superior starts making vague allusions to not being satisfied with the team spirit in the company. Instead of immediately assuming you are being criticized personally and feeling hurt, ask him a direct question: 'What exactly are you expecting from us? How do you want to see the situation improved?'

## Sales

A good strategy for selling your ideas is to ask questions. Without realizing what is happening your partner will frequently adopt your ideas as his own and naturally accept them.

Ask a potential client:

- 'What is your overriding objective? What do you want to achieve?'
- 'What is important to you?'
- 'What is your long-term strategy?'
- 'What priorities have you set?'
- 'What is your budget framework? What are you prepared to invest in terms of resources?'
- 'What advantages are you expecting from our cooperation?'
- 'What are you expecting of us?'
- 'Are there any special aspects I should take into account? Are there any restrictions I should know about?'

Take note of your client's replies, and make use of them in the following negotiations.

If the response is negative you can ask 'Have you ever made an exception?' List all the possible exceptions, and use them in the subsequent discussions with your client.

Angry clients can easily be calmed down by asking 'How can I be of assistance to you?'

## Unpleasantness

If you find the topic of a conversation uncomfortable you can ask 'Why do you say that?', or simply change the subject by asking a question about something else entirely.

To communicate better it is important to present your case convincingly and, if necessary, keep repeating your demands until you have achieved your objective. Exercises 3 and 5 should be of help to you.

## Organizational development

In her book *Creating Shared Vision*, consultant Marjorie Parker lists a number of examples of questions which she finds useful in helping managers to find a vision for their company:

- 'What is meaningful about your work?'
- 'What is meaningful about your contribution to this organization?'
- 'What contribution is your company making to society?'
- 'What difference does your company's efforts make?'
- 'What is your company especially good at?'
- 'How is your company distinctive and unique?'
- 'What added value do your company's customers receive?'
- 'Why are your company's customers demanding its products and services?'
- 'What makes your company different from others in the same industry?'
- 'How are you helping other company plants to become more successful?'

However, these questions alone will probably not encourage visions. To obtain a response from managers which are genuine reflections of their values, intuitive insights and imagination at some point in time in the future, the 'scene' has to be set. This is the most difficult part. The consultant can't just sit down and ask the manager questions and expect visions to emerge. In her book Marjorie Parker describes how she worked with the manager – and how being in a relaxed state and initiating guided imagery is crucial. Also, knowing which themes are central to the core of the organization/the organization's uniqueness. In addition, the desired time frame is important. In the case referred to in her book, the manager's responses were a result of envisioning the company as if it were already five years into the future. In other words, the questions themselves are not sufficient in visioning.

After you have created a clear and compelling vision of your organization you can pose the following questions:

- 'What are the appropriate structures, systems and skills for your organization?'
- 'How do they differ from your current structures, systems and skills?'
- 'What steps are necessary to move you from where you are today to that which you envisage?'

These are questions which managers need to address to make their visions a reality. The first two have to do with: given the kind of organization we envisage, what then are the structures, systems and skills which we need to develop to make our vision a reality? In other words, visions provide a framework which guide us in making choices today – choices which may entail new structures, systems and skills.

Based on what we envisage and an awareness of what we need to change in our current reality, then the third question is appropriate: 'What steps are necessary . . .'. This has to do with developing plans for action.

91

# Part IV—Participation

# 9 | Leadership style

A manager's leadership style determines the motivation of his staff. An authoritarian superior tells his subordinates precisely what to do, and describes in detail exactly how they should do it. Modern management theory teaches us that the staff should know what the objectives of the company are.

In this book I go a step further, and recommend that managers work out their objectives together with their staff, and then allow them as much freedom as possible within given guidelines so that they can decide for *themselves* how they are going to carry out their tasks. With the objective clearly in mind, they should be able to take the initiative themselves. Of course, this assumes they have the courage to take on responsibilities. Treating people pleasantly builds up self-confidence. On the other hand, a manager who is only interested in the figures on the annual balance sheet is not going to win the hearts of his staff.

An authoritarian leadership style is no longer in tune with the times. Nobody likes being ordered around all the time. But it is just as unsuitable to let go of the reins completely. If not enough demands are made, and the time is used for drinking coffee and having a leasurely smoke, the effect is just as demoralizing as that created by over-strict leadership. The challenge is to discover a having a leisurely smoke, the effect is just as demoralizing as that objectives, direct communication and participation. Human fellowship and mutual respect ensure a good working atmosphere.

## Ethical values

**95** | Morals are an authority forbidding, ordering and controlling. In contrast, ethics are founded on a deeply-rooted respect for the rights of others. Transferring these to the world of work gives two different management philosophies founded on different values: one is of giving orders and seeing they are carried out; the other is a democratic philosophy.

## Feelings

Ethical values are concerned with feelings, secret opinions and attitudes to others. Personal well-being is an important prerequisite for a good working atmosphere. However, many people claim that all this fuss about emotions is out of place at work. Here we are dealing with plain figures and unsentimental facts. Such people have not understood that human behaviour is guided not only by the brain, but also by the heart.

The following short example is typical. A middle-aged employee handed in his notice after working for the same firm for ten years, and applied for a better-paid job with another company. The main reason for his decision was not, however, money, nor a more interesting job, nor even increased status, but age-old conflicts with his immediate boss. This was revealed when, on receiving confirmation of the new job, he spontaneously cried: 'At last I'm getting away from Fred Mackintosh!'

The manager who fails to think about the kind of emotional reactions his behaviour might cause in others deprives himself of the possibility of getting closer to his staff as people.

The manager who purposely keeps his distance is often afraid that he will lose authority if he lets others get too close to him. Keeping people at a distance may well signify fear of one's own feelings. But it is essential to take the plunge and become more closely acquainted with one's strong and weak sides, and realize how one's own behaviour influences the attitudes of one's staff.

Feelings are only dangerous when they have to be suppressed. If, on the other hand, they can be allowed free rein without having to fear recriminations, the people concerned can start a dialogue, and this is the first step on the road to mutual understanding. In the course of such a conversation it may be revealed that the employee does not actually object to the contents of a decision, but has only reacted to the way they have been introduced. Perhaps he feels he has been overlooked, and finally wants an opportunity to make his opinion known.

## Openness

Openness means that it is acceptable to discuss controversial topics. Openness means that you are allowed to hold a different opinion. Openness also means that it is all right to show your feelings.

Openness does not mean being naive or spreading out your entire family history in front of all your colleagues. I myself decide which thoughts I wish to pass on to others and which I prefer to keep to myself.

I am also fully aware that my openness might be misused by others. If my heart is brimming over and my mouth follows suit, everything I say may well be used by others against me later. I present myself as a target for my opponent's sharpened arrows. But I take this risk consciously. Whatever happens, it is the lesser of two evils to be gossiped about than to bury everything deep down, and end up with a stiff neck or even an ulcer. Feelings need a vent.

Openness to everything happening everyday at the working place is a necessary precondition if the staff are to identify with the objectives of the company. But openness of this kind is not possible if the boss is not prepared to open up himself, to be available for others, and slough off the belief that distance from his staff is one of the pillars on which his authority rests.

The manager who is unable to empathize and always answers criticism with criticism is cutting the ground from beneath his feet, since fear of the boss's anger only results in indifference or, frequently, irrational modes of behaviour.

The head of a public service organization who was renowned for being excellent at his job but a very strict superior received a lot of complaints about the amount of time taken for work to be processed. On top of this, certain sets of documents actually disappeared. He asked his staff whether they were having problems with their work, and was told they were not. One day he could think of no other solution than to go through his assistants' desks at the end of the day. In the drawer of an older lady he discovered the missing documents. Some of them had been lying there untouched for more than six months. When he spoke to her about it, it became clear that she was afraid of making mistakes, but did not dare to ask questions either. Any tasks which she did not feel 100% sure about ended up in the drawer.

Without employees who are confident enough and willing to take responsibility it is impossible for the manager to achieve the results he needs for the advancement of his own career. Thus managers must learn to turn the negative emotional reactions of their staff into something constructive, and not just smoothe over conflicts by burying their heads in the sand.

The daily decisions a manager has to make are bound to produce opposing views, anger, or even aggression on the part of those affected. For this reason the management should try to preempt outbreaks of anger by considering in advance which individuals or groups will be affected, and providing them with information and the opportunity to discuss matters so as to create a basis for trust. If a case is too pressing to allow time for discussion, the manager should at least explain afterwards why he decided on one course of action or another.

If the manager shies away from the extra work involved in putting everybody in the picture, he should not be surprised if subsequently his staff are unwilling to support him to the very last. After all, it is only human to hold back from putting your heart and soul into something not in your own interests.

If the staff are forced to do something without actually being totally convinced they want to do it, emotional tension enters a relationship.

A conscientious person will try to remain loyal to his boss despite everything. But secretly he will feel his reluctance. His rebellious thoughts get into conflict with his adopted ideal of obedience. His secret aggression is treated as a forbidden feeling. It awakens feelings of guilt and is suppressed. A bad conscience ensues. Coming to terms with these ambivalent and confusing feelings takes time and energy, which detract from getting on with the work in hand.

Less conscientious employees express their reluctance more or less openly: they put certain things at the bottom of the pile, deal with private matters during working time, use the telephone a lot to call friends, take a good deal of sick leave, or carry on open sabotage.

Whatever the case may be, the manager ends up with a worse result than was necessary. This is the disadvantage of an authoritarian style of leadership. Open communication helps to avoid problems of this kind. And if they should really occur, the team itself will make sure that the damage is kept to a minimum.

In an open working atmosphere the department or group will try to find a common solution without creating a front in opposition to the boss, or always laying the blame at his door.

## Fear

Fear is a product of insecurity, and thus flourishes in a working atmosphere in which open communication is a rarity.

Decisions which are made without reference to the person affected are a threat to his reputation or his job, and therefore, by extension, to his economic situation, responsibility for his family, and career prospects.

In a situation permeated by fear the employee is understandably preoccupied with achieving his own security, or finding a way out, rather than achieving good results at work. Fear can thus have a crippling effect on the enthusiasm for work, on the wealth of initiative, and on efficiency.

Once fear and insecurity have taken root the danger is that they will keep growing, and also spread to other areas. The free flow of information can prevent such damaging developments. But for this the manager must be able to overcome his own fears.

Suppressed feelings take their revenge by creating fear. People simply do not want to be reminded about unpleasant experiences in their childhood or with a previous boss. Thus they develop a thick skin. The hard exterior is supposed to imply that inside everything is under control. But constantly wearing a mask takes a lot of energy. Some people clench their teeth so hard and for so long that they damage their jaws. Others get back pains because they literally cannot bear it any longer. Psychological stress can even cause such awful muscular pains in the legs that every step is agony. The solution is to embark on a course of physiotherapy. It is socially more acceptable to suffer from and treat a physical ailment than an emotional one.

A physiotherapist talks about her work: 'People get ill when they are either over- or under-stimulated. The results of this inner disharmony are headaches, migraine, stiff necks, backache, heart pains and anxiety. In the course of my work I constantly meet over-worked managers who do not realize that the company and the staff can only be successful if they work together, not against each other. The other group of patients are their employees, who are suffering from tension because their bosses never give them a chance to realize their potential at work. I am convinced that companies could save millions on sickness if they would only see the relationship between their employees' health and their abilities to realize their potential at work.'

Suppressed feelings are bad for your health and cripple your ability to act. Openness is the medicine. The first step is to confront unpleasant things in order to overcome fear. Only when I am prepared to look truth in the face and admit to my 'hateful' feelings will the tension be released and the process of reconciliation begin.

Being able to forgive is a sign of strength. Here and now I can take the decision to forgive my worst enemy, and in doing so relieve myself of a burden of negative feelings. It is not even necessary to inform him that I have come to terms with him emotionally.

**Morals and ethics**

99 | Every person is unique. For different individuals with varying

opinions, experiences and interests to be able to live together in peace as a family, a company or a state, they need norms and values which are respected by everyone.

Human behaviour is guided on the one hand by proscriptions and controls which have been drawn up by people or authorities with power over us, i.e. power to punish. A child is too small to differentiate between good and evil. Thus it trusts its parents to know why this or that is allowed or forbidden.

On the other hand, every person has the freedom of will to decide to do something or to leave it – and then to accept the consequences of his actions.

There is an enormous difference between someone doing something of his own free will or because he feels forced into it. The dichotomy of having to and wanting to can be described by the concepts 'morals' and 'ethics'.

In his article 'Psychoanalysis and Ethics', the Danish psychiatrist Henning Paikin writes:

> 'Morals are the norms someone draws on in a specific situation in order to call forth a certain action or mode of behaviour in someone else. Conversely, ethics are something much more deep-seated. Ethics are founded upon the humanistic idea that every person is irreplaceable and has the freedom to develop his personality. This conviction is only possible if everyone is able to experience in his life what it means to be free and able to act and thus on this basis to recognize what constitutes the freedom and independence of others.'

In this sense, morals are an authority which forbid, order and control. By contrast, ethics are founded on a deeply-rooted respect for the rights of others and belief in their ability and will to determine their actions themselves on the basis of a personal system of values.

If we transfer these ideas to the world of work we can differentiate between two management philosophies founded on quite different values.

The concept 'morals' is related to a leadership style characterized by giving orders and carefully checking that these orders are carried out. Communication is a one-way process: from top to bottom. Employees are passive order-takers. They can be moved around, or even replaced like figures on a chess board. They are expected to react obediently to orders from above. Using their brains or taking the initiative are not encouraged.

On the other hand, the concept 'ethics' reflects a democratic leadership style characterized by staff who are respected for thinking and acting independently – a valuable asset to the company. They contribute actively to the success of the company, and are thus given the opportunity to participate in the decision-making process. They are mainly motivated from within rather than as a result of external pressure. In this kind of working atmosphere control can gradually be replaced by self-control. To achieve optimum results the company invests not only in machines and equipment, but also in the development of people.

In this context it is important to differentiate between an authoritarian personality and a person with authority. I use the phrase 'authoritarian leadership style' to indicate that power is vested in a certain person or title. A person with authority, by contrast, is influential because of their professional and human qualities. He or she is convincing, can motivate people and make them enthusiastic.

An authoritarian personality forces his will on others. A person with authority stimulates others to take responsibility themselves. A manager should always be an authority his staff can look up to.

## Authoritarian leadership is only effective in the short term

Well-being and efficiency are closely related. This is an important message for anyone who believes that they are being most efficient when they take all the decisions on their own. Managers are on the wrong track if they think they can treat their staff just as the fancy takes them, because growing unemployment will ensure that they buckle down and do as they are told.

If dissatisfaction amongst the employees increases it is always the company that loses in the end – whether the staff go or stay.

Creative people want to decide for themselves. If decisions are constantly taken for them they feel they are being personally denigrated: 'The manager doesn't value my work', 'That lot up there are so taken up with themselves that they're totally in-different to my opinion', 'The boss doesn't trust me.'

'OK, tit for tat. Why should I make a special effort for the firm if the firm is not the least interested in me and my needs? Your objective is no longer my objective. If my boss refuses to recognize my achievement, I'll find it elsewhere. I'll spare myself for my leisure activities and family, and have a look round for another employer who does value my work.'

Even during periods of high unemployment well-qualified, experienced employees will always find a new job, and with them the company loses their expertise.

But even with those who stay because they are too old, or do not have the right qualifications, the company will not have an easy time – frustration ruins the working mood.

*Dissatisfaction leads to inner detachment*  Orders from above are only accepted grudgingly. Depending on the actual power structures, an employee can choose open or more clandestine forms of resistance. Protests and strikes are the most visible expression of discontent. A private work-to-rule campaign is much less obvious, but often just as effective in reducing productivity. The same is true of frequent absence due to illness. Secret anger can fester just below the surface for years before a suitable occasion causes it to break out in an explosive release of emotion. Everyone is amazed because there was no relation between the actual catalyst and the severity of the explosion. Nobody else had noticed how much anger and frustration had been building up over the years.

If dissatisfaction is a long-term experience many people start to become resigned to it. Inner detachment becomes a fact. People continue to draw their salaries, arrive punctually for work and leave on the dot, but otherwise only do what is absolutely unavoidable. The rest of the time is spent complaining how awful everything is: 'There's no point in discussing it with a manager like him. Either he doesn't have any time or else everything goes in one ear and out the other.'

Take the following quotation from a private letter written during office hours:

> 'I'm sitting here at the office with my best conscientious face on, but I can't get involved in what I'm doing although it really ought to interest me. My thoughts are elsewhere.'

It would be worth researching into the degree of lost productivity occurring every day in departments and offices throughout the country just because the staff refuse to give of their very best.

Pressure from above only increases the will to achieve in the short-term. To lead to permanent results a manager has to take his staff's needs into account. A good working atmosphere where people can have a laugh together and sometimes agree to differ creates a positive attitude to work.

The price the manager has to pay for participation is a longer decision-making process. You need time if everyone is going to be allowed to express their point of view. And perhaps previously hidden differences of opinion and conflicts will emerge for everyone to see. Nevertheless, a decision which involves the staff in active participation will be given much greater support when put into practice than a lone decree from the top.

If employees are excluded from the decision-making process it is superficially quicker. However, it can subsequently take ages to turn a decision into action, because when the staff defend themselves like hedgehogs the manager is in danger of getting caught on their spines.

*Sham democracy*   Sham democracy is when the manager asks his staff to come to a discussion so as to talk about a problem on which he has already taken a decision. It is even worse when, after lengthy debate, the team does reach a decision only to find that afterwards the boss has changed everything without giving any reasons to anyone.

The board of a society met to decide on dates for the next six months. After a session lasting three hours everyone was in agreement. Subsequently, the chairman took it upon himself to change the programme. His behaviour gave the others the feeling that they had wasted their time. Gradually, no-one was willing to spend time working for the society. At this point the chairman complained how lazy the members were. He had not realized that it was his own behaviour which had caused the others to adopt a passive attitude.

Similar cases occur at work every day. Of course, the manager has the right to decide what he thinks best. He does not always have to call a meeting before taking a decision, but if he asks the staff for their opinion and then ignores it he should at least explain why.

The staff in the psychiatric department of a hospital always emphasized team-work. Together they decided how to solve a particular problem. But the psychiatric consultant took absolutely no notice of what had been suggested, and did something else altogether.

With justification, the staff felt they had been passed over. Nobody objected to the fact that the boss had chosen a different solution; but if he had really taken cooperation seriously he would have informed the group that he had changed his opinion. The decision (i.e. the end-product) would have been the same, but the decision-finding (i.e. the procedure) would have found more support among his staff. The team would have been on his side instead of falling in with him, but frustrated and bearing him a secret grudge.

A manager has to make sure that his or her words are reflected in deeds. Otherwise, there is a constant air of confusion among staff which can easily lead to misunderstandings. Office gossip is one of the frequent results of discovering that all those wonderful phrases about humanity, ethical values and company identity are completely divorced from company reality.

Information and open communication, even with regard to unpleasant matters, are the best method of combatting rumours. But the information must flow in both directions: the manager must ensure that everyone knows what is planned, and why. The staff must inform their boss if there is something likely to prevent them from fulfilling their objectives. Unfortunately, not all managers value suggestions for improvement made by their staff. Many good ideas never reach the ears of the Managing Director because the heads of department leave them on their desks collecting dust.

## Middle management as a barrier to communication

Middle management frequently acts as a buffer between top level management and clerical staff. Those at the top expect to be able to carry on their important business undisturbed, and thus assume middle management will absorb any staff complaints half-way. But the rank and file are not satisfied with complaining; they want to introduce improvements. The head of a department often fails to notice the difference, and initially blocks their progress, just to be on the safe side.

The negative attitude of many middle managers to suggestions for change is not, however, just a problem of personality. It is also a structural problem. In an organization constructed on hierarchical lines there is always a group of people in the middle whose primary duty is to check that others are doing their jobs properly, rather than achieving results themselves. If this supervisors' control consists of pedantically scrutinizing every tiny detail and screaming out loud every time he finds the smallest formal mistake, the staff soon lose their motivation.

In this context, the following complaints can often be heard:

- 'My head of department pokes his nose into everything. He wastes his time quibbling. If I write "and so on", for example, he corrects it to "etc". Our whole middle management is pretty unproductive.'
- 'In our company the bureaucracy's awful. Every suggestion is checked by at least ten supervisors before it's accepted. Work's no fun under those conditions.'
- 'If I take the initiative in something all I get to hear is: it's not your baby.'
- 'My suggestions frequently end up on my boss's desk. I can't get any further than that with my good ideas.'

Middle management itself is stuck between two stools. The chances of promotion to a higher post are often negligible. The top managers are not going to move from where they are; lower down the scale, ambitious colleagues are already in the starting blocks, threatening one's own position. Blocking suggestions for improvement is thus an act of self-defence. While behaviour of this kind is understandable from the point of view of the individual, it has a destructive effect on the motivation of the staff. They feel as though they are hitting their heads against a brick wall. They try it once or twice and then give up. There is no point.

How can one help middle management out of their dilemma? The answer is: better training, alternative career paths, i.e. the possibility of earning a good salary in professional positions without responsibility for personnel, and softening the hierarchical structures within companies in favour of more project work and self-regulating groups.

### Self-realization through participation

The manager who gives his staff the opportunity to participate actively in what is going on not only ensures that he has access to important information; he can also be assured of his staff's loyalty. Participation increases people's commitment and reduces their desire to argue. Thus, the clever manager thinks of his staff in terms of a set of resources. A particular employee is better acquainted with his particular field than anyone else, and is the first to recognize what could be improved.

Participation in what is going on means possibilities for self-realization. Having this human need fulfilled is very motivating. The employees' ideal shopping-list includes the following points:

- 'Increase your staff's willingness to work hard by giving them more responsibility.'
- 'Draw your staff into the discussion before you decide on innovations, and don't wait until afterwards when it's too late to change anything.'
- 'Listen to what your staff have to say and take their wishes into account. Avoid giving them the feeling that you're indifferent to them.'
- 'Give your staff a chance to participate in designing their job-description.'

Participation is also a panacea for conflicts, especially as many conflicts are nothing more than a defiant reaction to the unpleasant feeling of not being of any significance in the eyes of the boss. 'If you're not going to take any notice of me of your own free will, I'll just have to make you.'

I was once contracted by a political party to take responsibility for the organizational preparation and execution of a large conference. My only guidelines were: this time everything should be different from usual.

I suggested that the delegates should discuss the topics in groups first before considering them in plenary session. At the beginning everyone was very sceptical ('Can we risk it?'), but they did eventually accept my suggestion half-heartedly. We came to a compromise: half the topics were supposed to be discussed and approved in groups first, the other half were to come straight before the plenary session.

We divided the 180 delegates into 15 groups, with 12 members each, and I spent two days training the group leaders in motivating and creative methods of work.

At the conference everything went just as I had predicted. The topics which had been discussed in groups first were subsequently passed by the plenary session without difficulty. Even in the groups which had not managed to get finished there was a harmonious atmosphere, and considerable trust in the group leader: 'We trust you to represent our interests correctly.' Everyone was in a good mood, everyone felt they belonged to their group, and when the conference came to an end, everyone agreed that the groupwork had been the best part of the conference.

In the case of those topics which had not first been discussed in groups, there was a good deal of dissent during the plenary session. It led to those endless monologues by people who always hold forth at length, to people consciously talking at cross purposes, and to those rounds of heated voting for which politics is so noted.

The working methods a manager chooses determine the results he can achieve. If the staff are drawn into the decision-making process right from the beginning, the chances are that when the decisions are later put into practice friction can be kept to a minimum. Participation engenders a feeling of belonging. In this book I use the word 'participation' in the sense of individual employees having the opportunity to take part in what is going on. Thus I go a step further than formal worker participation as defined by the unions, which are supposed to represent the interests of all workers. In my definition participation is related to direct democracy, while worker participation is more a form of representative democracy at work.

At the end of this book there are a number of working methods which achieve staff participation while being structured in such a way that really effective work can be done. The techniques are suitable both for organizational development and for the in-house training of managers and staff.

# 10 | Delegating

Management means achieving results through other people. The ability to motivate your staff is the most important quality a good manager can possess. Delegating responsibility is the key to success.

## What is delegation?

Delegation might be described as transferring precisely defined tasks from a higher to a lower level: from the Managing Director to his deputy, from the head of a section to the head of a sub-section, from a personal assistant to a secretary. This is the way in which superiors buy time for leadership, i.e. for developing strategies and determining the paths which will lead to the goals set.

Most employees are keen to take on more responsibility:

'More delegation would increase efficiency. Frequently responsibility rests with far too few people who, with the best will in the world, cannot possibly keep track of everything that is going on. We employees want more responsibility because then our work is more interesting.'

A failure to delegate means the superior is in danger of getting caught up in the details of an operation and losing his overview of the whole. Routine work takes the upper hand. The boss carries out the individual tasks himself instead of managing his staff. 'How' becomes more important than 'what', i.e. procedural regulations become an end in themselves. No-one poses questions such as 'What was actually the point of this regulation in the first place?'. They simply tick over as they have always done. Flexibility suffers, and the company gets sluggish.

Delegation must be voluntary. There is no point in trying to force it on a dictator against his will. The manager himself has to recognize the advantages, and mentally come to terms with the fact that his change in attitude towards his staff might turn into a painful process. It is never easy to take leave of old ideas, but it is well worth the effort. The staff achieving good results is a compliment to the boss.

### Seven excuses for avoiding delegation

Everybody is in favour of it – so long as talk of delegating responsibility is general and not binding. As soon as matters get serious, managers become extremely creative in trying to prove that it really does not work in practice. The seven most frequent excuses are:

- The staff already have far too much to do.
- The staff are not able to do it.
- The staff do not want to do it.
- I have nobody to delegate work to.
- I do not have the authority to do it.
- I do not have time to explain it.
- It is better if I do it myself.

*The staff already have far too much to do*   Concern for the staff's workload is the most common argument against having to delegate. For example:

- 'The staff should not be burdened with any more work.'
- 'Everyone already has far too much to do.'
- 'I am scared of demanding too much of the staff. Thus I would rather drown in work myself.'
- 'The staff are so over-burdened with work that I simply don't have the heart to push more onto them, even though there are tasks which could be delegated profitably.'
- 'There are times when the staff are under such pressure that I prefer to do it myself.'
- 'My staff don't have time to learn new things or take on extra work.'

Unwillingness to delegate would appear to hail from the most honourable motives – concern for the well-being of the staff. But only very few managers take the trouble to find out why their staff are drowning in work, and whether they are actually grateful for this concern.

A company constantly under pressure is frequently the victim of poor planning and inappropriate working routines. In cases like this, thorough tidying-up is long overdue anyway.

Managers and their staff often have quite different ways of interpreting situations. While the boss thinks he is doing his staff a favour by coping with everything on his own, the staff are frustrated because their work does not allow them sufficient opportunity for self-realization.

The following questions can be most helpful in uncovering what people really think and feel:

- Is there the right balance between your workload and your work capacity?
- Is the work you have to do commensurate with your qualifications?
- Do you have enough/too much/too little to do?
- Do you need to be relieved of tasks?
- Do the substitution routines function well?
- Do you think there is a need for in-service training? If so, specify.

*The staff are not able to do it* Many managers are unwilling to delegate because they fear their staff are not up to the task. This attitude creates a vicious circle: the manager does not delegate because the staff are not sufficiently knowledgeable. To become more knowledgeable they have to learn more. The boss does not have time to teach them. He is unable to teach them because he is so over-worked himself. He is so over-worked himself because he fails to delegate.

Most people have far greater potential than they usually reveal during an ordinary working day. Encourage your staff to continue developing their abilities, and use them in the interests of their own well-being as well as that of the company. In this context, confidence and self-confidence are key concepts.

Delegation is an excellent form of on-the-job training. Constantly having to apply one's knowledge to new challenges is not only a pre-condition for carrying out tasks satisfactorily, it is also an important motivating factor. Most people are keen to learn something new. Improved training increases both their self-confidence and their degree of personal involvement. The gain in productivity thus achieved far exceeds the costs of personnel development.

The following questions may help you to determine training requirements:

- In which fields would you like to improve your knowledge?
- Do you feel your superior expects too much/too little of you?
- What do you consider are your training needs?
- Should any of your duties be transferred to a higher/lower level? If so, which?

*The staff don't want to do it*   If an employee shows no interest at all in taking on extra tasks, or different ones, it can be assumed that he is afraid of the responsibility. Acting independently and taking the initiative always involves the risk of getting something wrong. Help your staff to be more self-confident. Give them the opportunity to learn from their mistakes. One peccadillo should not mark the end of someone's career.

If your staff do not seem to want to be bothered, try to find out why:

- Could it be that your own leadership style kills initiative?
- Is everybody so afraid of you that no-one dares to open their mouth?
- Has everybody really understood the objectives? Do not hesitate to explain your intentions again.
- Are there conflicts amongst colleagues due to poorly-defined areas of competence?
- Do your staff lack self-confidence: can I really risk doing that? What will the others have to say about it?
- Are your staff afraid that they are not adequately qualified for dealing with new tasks?

*I have nobody to delegate work to*   Delegation means distributing responsibility so that everyone knows what everyone else is doing, and so that decision-making is transferred to as low a level as possible. Thus understood, delegation is always an advantage irrespective of the number of people employed by a company.

A lack of staffing is not an argument against delegation. A critical assessment of the entire organization will help you to bring job assignment and routines into line with what is actually possible within the company.

The administrative value analysis (see exercise 27 at the end of the book) can be effective in improving efficiency in the company. Ask the following questions:

- Which tasks and routines are superfluous?
- Which tasks can be reduced in scope?
- What can be done differently in future?
- How can we increase productivity?

*I don't have the authority*   If the number of complaints about lack of authority to take responsibility for decisions grows noticeably, this indicates that tasks and responsibility are not in tune with one another. The objectives are often unclear to the individual sections. Typical complaints include:

- 'Our organizational chart does not correspond to reality.'
- 'It's quite unclear to me who is responsible for what, and to whom I could actually delegate something.'

To achieve a better overview of individual spheres of responsibility and the authority attached to them, ask the following questions:

- Is your job assignment in tune with your authority?
- Would you like to be given more authority in negotiating with clients? In which fields?
- Is it clear who is authorized to sign what?
- Which matters would you like to be authorized to sign yourself? What would be the consequences of this?

*I don't have time to explain it*   Many managers claim they do not have time to explain things:

- 'It's much quicker if I do it myself.'
  'If I have to explain how to do something first in minute detail it frequently takes longer than if I do it quickly myself.'

If you are always running to catch up with yourself there is probably something wrong with your personal efficiency and planning. How long have you left awkward tasks lying untouched on your desk? How often have you dedicated yourself heart and soul to routine work so as to avoid a difficult issue? You might very well be surprised if you take the trouble to write down what you actually spend your time doing.

Keep track of yourself over the period of a week or a month: What tasks do I carry out? How much time do I need for the various tasks? For example:

- routine administration.
- target and strategy development.
- crisis management.
- disseminating information.
- writing reports, statistics.
- training.
- representation.

- social contact with the staff.
- meetings.
- conferences and travel.

Many managers are firmly convinced that they spend most of their time working on strategy or solving acute crises. A time study of this kind helps to reveal that they actually spend most of their time dealing with routine tasks which might be delegated very profitably.

*It's better if I do it myself*   Delegation is based on trust. But some managers only feel secure when they do everything themselves. There are many reasons for not wanting to let go of the reins: a straightforward striving for power, fear of competition, or of seeming high-handed.

Typical comments by this group include:

- 'The fact that I'm the only one capable of doing this work gives me power.'
- 'If I were to delegate my work to others I'd become redundant.'
- 'I don't feel happy about pushing off less interesting tasks on others.'
- 'All of us here are equal. I can't give the others all the boring work while keeping the interesting stuff for myself.'
- 'I don't want my staff to think I'm high-handed.'
- 'If I have the time I prefer to do it myself.'

Managers who always do everything themselves are in danger of ruining their health while their staff sit around twiddling their thumbs. One nurse reports: 'We often get managers brought onto the ward with heart attacks. Some of them arrive at the hospital with their attaché cases, mobile telephones and lap-tops. Once they've been sent home they're back in no time at all with heart attack number two.'

Some workaholics pay for their lack of trust in their staff with their lives.

**The responsibility rests with the boss**

The responsibility always rests with the boss, even when the work is done by others. Thus delegation should only ever be introduced according to a carefully considered plan. And a superior is always well-advised to enquire regularly how the work is going.

112

Delegation presupposes confidence both in oneself and in others. As such, a superior has to take the risk that his trust might be misused, or that the task might not be carried out satisfactorily. Even in this case, the one who has delegated is answerable to the next higher authority. It does not make a very good impression to blame one's staff when a plan has misfired.

Responsibility for the following tasks rests with the superior:

- formulating objectives and strategies and motivating the staff;
- defining problems. Agreeing with the staff to what extent they themselves can choose the means by which objectives are achieved. Deciding on a regulatory framework. To be considered: the greater the leeway, the greater the creativity. Never losing control. Ensuring the flow of information upwards;
- defining precisely which results should be achieved. Potential objections should be aired in advance. Unity of purpose;
- agreeing on the period of time needed to complete tasks or achieve sub-objectives. This also means defining clear priorities;
- ensuring that the person who is supposed to carry out a task has enough authority and resources to do so;
- keeping people informed, giving advice and feedback, showing an interest.

**Tasks which can be delegated**

To discover what you can delegate it is worth drawing up a list covering all the tasks you carry out in the course of a month or a year. Also, write down how much time you need to deal with these tasks. Then draw up a second list noting the important tasks which are neglected because you do not have enough time to deal with them.

If there is a big discrepancy between what you should be doing and what you actually do, you are probably not getting your priorities right. It is high time you started concentrating on essentials, and letting others take on the remaining tasks.

Generally speaking, the following tasks might well be delegated:

- routine tasks.
- meetings and conferences.
- the boss's favourite jobs.
- special tasks.

- disseminating information and contact with clients.
- particularly time-consuming tasks.

*Routine tasks*  Routine work is composed of tasks which have to be done every day, but which are so standardized that they do not require much thought because they always recur in the same form.

*Meetings and conferences*  Every superior knows this dilemma: the need to represent the company to the outside world means attending conferences and a good deal of travel. Yet to motivate the staff he or she should spend as much time at the office as possible. The degree to which the staff are willing to get involved depends on the boss being available. However, many managers spend most of their time sitting in meetings while the files of unfinished work pile up on their desks.

Thus every superior should be absolutely honest with himself, and try to find out whether his presence at a conference is really essential, or whether he might not be represented by another member of staff. How often is a business trip really an excuse for getting away from the office?

Apart from anything else, delegating the task of attending meetings and conferences has the following advantages for the company:

- The member of staff who is allowed to travel finds the experience stimulating. When he comes back he is bubbling over with new ideas and develops his own initiatives.
- Being allowed to represent the boss at meetings and conferences is a sign of trust, and may constitute a reward for earlier achievements.
- Travel abroad is a kind of gratuity strengthening the employee's commitment to the company.
- Attending conferences increases professional and social competence. Getting to know new people, making contacts and building up a social network can be of great importance.
- The company is assured of better continuity. There is always someone around who can leap in if the boss is ill, has an accident or is on holiday.

*The boss's favourite jobs*  The boss's favourite jobs are the tasks he is best at. Perhaps it was due to his competence in these particular areas that he was promoted in the first place.

Take a hold on yourself, and delegate your favourite jobs to others, even if they take longer to do them than you would. A manager should be a manager and not a super administrative assistant.

If the manager is spending his time on the wrong things he is costing the company money. Resources are being used inappropriately if the boss spends his highly-paid time carrying out tasks which could be done just as well, or even better, by lower ranking staff.

Staff learn by experience. Give them the opportunity to develop their professional potential.

When the boss is absent his staff can represent him.

*Special tasks*  Special, time-consuming tasks which might be usefully delegated include writing reports, preparing statistical analyses, gathering background material on something, or revising the annual report.

*Information and contact with clients*  Disseminating information and contact with clients on a regular basis can be delegated. Staff who are in daily contact with clients anyway can also be entrusted with the task of informing them about new products or services. By talking to the client directly they are frequently made aware of complaints or existing needs. If they then pass these market indicators on to their boss, they strengthen the company's ability to adapt to changes in the environment in good time.

It is usually very motivating if members of staff who are usually isolated behind their desks are given the opportunity to make direct contact with clients.

When dealing with the media it is important that the company speaks with one voice. In really important matters the top manager should be the one to face the outside world. Over and above this, however, there are a number of in-house developments which may be of interest to the public, and even create a better image for the company. In such cases, an administrative assistant might also report on his or her own work. But in this context it is essential that the borders are clearly drawn, and authority properly allocated. The management should always be informed first.

*Particularly time-consuming tasks*  Something which constitutes boring routine work to the manager may well be a challenge to a member of staff, doing it for the first time. The boss gains time, the employee learns something new.

**Tasks which cannot be delegated**

The following tasks should not be delegated:

115  – responsibility for objectives and strategy.

- representation on particular occasions.
- key staff appointments.
- crisis management.
- company secrets.

*Responsibility for objectives and strategy* Responsibility for objectives and strategy lies with the top manager of a company. He can, of course, seek the assistance and advice of others, but he can never unload the responsibility on them. Even if he is the victim of bad advice, he is the one who has to face the music when the catastrophe has broken.

Leadership means pointing out the direction and convincing staff that this is the right path so that they will keep to it loyally. If everyone is fully cognisant of the overriding objective and the relevant terms of reference, there is no reason why the employees themselves should not choose the means to achieve that objective.

*Representation on special occasions* On particularly formal or important occasions the top manager cannot avoid being the one to represent the company. On these occasions it is the position and title of the person holding the address which is uppermost, i.e. it is often more important who says what than what they actually say. Examples include the official opening ceremonies of new facilities, retirement parties for long-serving staff, or especially important receptions.

*Key staff appointments* The appointment of staff to key positions has such far-reaching consequences for the company that the superior would be well advised to be involved himself. The wrong decision might prove extremely costly for the company.

In cases of disciplinary action the authority of the superior is essential.

*Crisis management* When there is a crisis the manager himself must be the one to lead the team dealing with it. The best method is to develop a strategy during a quiet period outlining what has to be done in a crisis. This means a well-defined allocation of tasks and responsibilities, address lists, telephone numbers and alternative means of communication in case the telephone switchboard stops functioning, or the computer goes on strike.

Draw up clear guidelines specifying who is allowed to state the company's case at press conferences with journalists, the radio and television. For particularly important questions it can only be the top manager or his second-in-command who appear in public.

*Company secrets* If a company tries to adopt a policy of open communication it automatically follows that there should be as little secrecy as possible in internal matters. This is especially relevant in relation to setting company objectives and policy. The stamp of confidentiality means precisely that the information is supposed to be restricted to a small circle of initiates.

It is quite a different matter when it comes to information such as details of technical procedures and research findings reaching outsiders. As few people as possible should be privy to company secrets of this kind, especially as industrial espionage is rife.

# Part V—Practical activities for personal and organizational development

# Practical activities for personal and organizational development

This part of the manual is designed to help you to make the important step from the 'what' to the 'how'. Section 1, 'Personal mastery', contains exercises that will help improve communication skills, since the best idea is of little value if you don't succeed in convincing others and putting it into practice. For establishing a rapport it is useful to learn the techniques of active listening, asking questions, and giving and receiving positive as well as negative feedback. The biggest challenge, however, is to learn to talk about difficult matters and still remain friends. Therefore a couple of exercises for conflict solving are included.

Section 2, 'Visions, goals and strategy', is designed to help in the creation of shared visions, and to tackle the frustration which might occur in the period between getting the vision clear and turning it into reality. Exercises are also included on how to design a strategy, set priorities and develop a plan of action.

Section 3, 'Organizational development', contains working methods for organizational transformation through teamwork. By focusing on potential instead of limitations, noting expectations and agreeing on the rules in advance, misunderstandings can be avoided later. Advice on how to make teamwork function and how to involve employees in saving money for the company is also given.

# 1—Personal mastery

# 2—Visions, goals and strategy

# 3—Organizational development

# 1 | Personal mastery

The exercises in this section correspond with Part III of this book, *Free and Open Communication*. The ability to deal with all kinds of people is your basic qualification as a leader. Communication skills are essential for motivating staff. Trouble must be taken to find out what is really wanted, and then to make the message clear. Personal mastery is an ongoing process. Learning goes on as long as you live – and that is what makes life so fascinating. Good luck!

# Clear communication

**Goals**

The following checklist will help to bring clarity into a discussion or written communication.

**Possible snags**

Many people are not aware of their own goals. As a consequence, they are unable to communicate clearly. The receiver has no chance of understanding the message and acting accordingly. This, again, might result in disappointment on behalf of the sender, who feels that his own needs are not being satisfied. Many accusations of discrimination are really a matter of misunderstanding because the 'victim' did not express his or her wishes clearly. Women especially have a great deal to learn concerning direct communication. They need more courage to state what they want, and stop expecting other people to read their thoughts. ('I wish you understood what I really meant when I didn't say anything.')

Many managers describe their goals deliberately in well-rounded formulations, because the less concrete they are the easier it will be to obtain agreement. The same is even more true for politicians. 'Freedom' is a word everybody can agree on in principle. Trouble starts when we go to the heart of the matter: 'Freedom for whom?' 'Freedom to do what?' etc.

By consciously choosing unclear formulations the manager is cheating himself. Even if a decision can be taken with a minimum of time, conflicts will arise when words are translated into action: some employees may not understand what the manager really means, others discover too late that the decision is not in their own interests, and start sabotaging. Therefore it is worth investing time in making the message clear and getting consensus.

The following checklist is inspired by Genie Z. Laborde's *Influencing with Integrity*, though all examples are my own.

When hearing/using a noun, ask the question 'What?' for clarification. Verbs invite the question 'How?'. Generalizations (always, never) are usually unsuitable. Ask yourself the question 'Are you really sure?' Norms (should, shouldn't, must, mustn't) often kill creativity. Allow yourself to be rebellious by asking the question 'What if I don't?' Finally, comparatives (better, easier) are often used to unite a disparate group of people to reach a goal without having to state clearly what exactly the goal is. Ask for clarification: 'Better than what?', 'What do you mean by better?'

Examples:

- Noun: e.g. 'efficiency'.
  Ask for clarification: '*What* exactly do you mean by 'efficiency'?'

  The same word can mean completely different things to different people. By asking a clarifying question misunderstandings can be avoided. The description 'an assertiveness course' might spark off, amongst others, the following associations: 'a course for frustrated women', 'domination techniques', 'a course on grousing', 'a course on communicating', 'personal mastery', 'a course at a low level', 'a management course'. Thus it is important to ask: 'What do you mean when you refer to an "assertiveness course"?'
- Verb: e.g. 'sharpening ourselves up'.
  Ask for clarification: '*How* are we supposed to do that?'

  It is tempting to come up with fine-sounding but non-committal statements about what we should all be doing without the person making the statement actually having thought his ideas through. By agreeing on the 'how', subsequent conflicts can be avoided.
- Generalization: e.g. 'always', 'never', 'You always arrive late for meetings', or 'You never have time'.
  Ask for clarification: 'Is it really true that I always/never . . .?'

  By asking the speaker to be more *precise*, he or she is made aware that they are exaggerating. The words 'always' and 'never' are seldom accurate (cf. exercise 2).
- Norms: e.g. 'should', 'must', 'ought to'.
  Ask a *contradictory question*: 'What if I won't? What if it doesn't work? Can we find other ways of doing it?'

  An implicit reference to existing norms (must, must not, should, should not, ought to) can prove obstructive when thinking on new lines: 'We do what we have always done because that is simply what "one" does.' To release creativity, allow yourself to be somewhat provocative by asking 'What if it can't?' Perhaps new paths leading to your goal can thus be discovered.
- Comparatives: e.g. 'better', 'easier', 'We ought to be better human beings'.
  Ask for clarification: 'What *exactly* is meant by better? Should women stay at home in order better to look after their children, or should they become managers so as to create a better working environment in which people feel

better and achieve better efficiency, or should they become involved in politics to create a better society?'

Imprecise formulations like 'better' can be legitimized by a politician wanting to gather together a disparate group of people (all Europeans) to aim for a common goal (a better future). By using loose formulations in combination with setting objectives, we are able to smoothe over areas of possible disunity only to find that conflicts return like a boomerang when we reach the stage of turning words into actions. Only then, when ideas are supposed to be put into practice, does it become clear that we all have a completely different conception of what 'better' is.

## Exercise 2 | I-Messages

### Goals
This exercise is designed to help one say what is really meant, and to pass on constructive criticism.

### Possible snags
This is not an ego-trip: only 'I' am allowed to make demands. 'I' am always right. Of course, I am allowed to express my needs, but so too are others. Consider the consequences of your actions.

The I-message technique is the brain-child of Dr Thomas Gordon, and is described in his book *Leader Effectiveness Training (LET)*. I was inspired by his work to develop the following exercise. All the examples derive from my own experience as a management consultant.

This exercise can be carried out alone or together with others.

### Individually

Write down on a piece of paper what you usually say when you are angry with someone. Then reformulate your sentences according to the following pattern.

### As a group

One after the other, give an example of how you usually hide what you really mean or feel, and how you criticize others. Then reformulate your sentence according to the following pattern.

## A word to the trainer

Create a safe atmosphere where nobody is afraid of making a fool of himself, and help the group members to find the right level of openness. If nobody dares to open his mouth there will be no learning. On the other hand, some participants might be tempted to take up intimate family matters and then regret it later. Motivate the group members to share experiences which everybody can learn from, but make it clear that everybody is himself responsible for the degree of his own self-disclosure. For example:

| Expressing displeasure | I-message |
|---|---|
| This work is lousy. | Perhaps I didn't make myself quite clear, what I am really after is . . . I assumed that you . . . Now I am disappointed because . . . Next time, I should be grateful if . . . |
| You get on my nerves. | I'm feeling irritable today. |

| Generalizing | I-message |
|---|---|
| Nobody ever tells us anything. | I'd like to be informed regularly about xyz and especially to what extent it affects me personally. |
| | It's very difficult for me to do my work properly if I don't know what is supposed to be going on in my field. |
| | I feel insecure when I don't know what's going on. |
| You never pass on feedback. | I'd be grateful if you'd have a look at this piece of work and tell me what you think of it. It's important to me. |
| You're always criticizing. | I'd be grateful if you'd tell me what you like about this piece of work and where I could improve it. |
| You always do everything yourself. | I'd be grateful if you'd delegate this task to me. |
| John Smith is always getting permission to travel to courses and conferences abroad. | I should like to take part in xyz course. |

| | |
|---|---|
| You leave your things lying all over the place. | I get the impression that you don't take me and my work seriously when you leave your clothes lying all over the house. Please hang them up in the cupboard. |
| **Attacking**<br>You're a tyrant | **I-message**<br>I want an active role in what's going on. |
| You never take any notice of anyone. | I want you to . . . |
| You're always so negative. | I didn't realize you'd take it that way. Let me explain. I did xyz because . . . |
| **Making someone look ridiculous**<br>I suppose you're a man-hater? | **I-message**<br>I don't understand the purpose of assertiveness courses for women. I'm curious. Please explain to me what you do at these seminars, and why you don't want any men present. |

**Exercise 3**

# Convincing others

**Goals**

This exercise demonstrates how you can build up what you want to say so that you will be heard. Thus the objective is to get someone to do what you want them to do. This is important in sales situations, or when you want to convince another person to accept your suggestions.

**Possible snags**

The worst pitfall is poor preparation. You have to invest time in considering fully *what* you want to say, *how* you want to say it, *who* will be affected, and *whose support* you require.

### 1 Preparation

Good preparation is the key to success. If there is a new and important item you wish to discuss at a meeting do not wait until the meeting itself before introducing it. Make sure you win allies in advance who are willing to support you.

Remember: Every new idea passes through three phases:

(1) Not being taken notice of or made to look ridiculous.
(2) Being actively opposed.
(3) Being accepted as perfectly obvious.

By trying out your ideas on your unofficial network before you present them formally, you can test reactions. You might get new ideas or see new angles you can integrate in your proposition – and the other players have an opportunity to get used to your idea.

Think about *how* you are going to say something as well as *what* you are going to say. The best ideas are of no use if you cannot manage to present them so that your listeners will be convinced.

Highly trained people are used to thinking analytically, and frequently express themselves in the abstract. By restricting your presentation to a straightforward analysis of facts and figures you may well emphasize the intellectual level, but your listeners will often remain untouched by your proposition. You are only appealing to the head and not to the heart.

To win people over you have to emphasize the emotional content of your proposition. This can be achieved by taking your own experience as a starting point, and describing what you felt in a special situation. Do not be afraid of showing your human side.

Use pictorial language, as though your listeners were watching a film while hearing you speak. Create mental images by appealing to the senses: describe details so that your listeners can see, hear, feel, smell and taste.

Particularly when you are forced to present a lot of figures, it is important to use examples and comparisons which people can recognize and identify with.

Vary your voice. Speak clearly and articulate well. Make sure your body language corresponds to what you are saying. The unconscious signals broadcast by your facial expressions and posture will immediately reveal whether or not you believe in what you are saying.


## 2 Presentation

Good presentation is like a three-course dinner. First you titillate the palate with an appetizer, then comes the main course, and finally the dessert.

Step 1  *Establish rapport and analyse the situation ('appetizer')*
Try your best to ensure you are on the same wavelength as your customer/boss/audience. A Native American proverb says that you can't understand another person before you have walked in his moccasins. So put on your customer's shoes. Try to see the world through his glasses. Establish rapport. The better you manage to take a starting point in the other person's interests, the more he will listen to you.

Find out what the situation is by answering the following questions:

– What is the current situation for my customer/boss/audience, etc?
– What is the problem? What is not the problem?
– How can I define and encapsulate what is supposed to be done?
– What is it all about? Are there any hidden agendas? Who is involved? Who will be affected personally?
– What happened? What might happen in future?
– What will be the consequences? For whom? When? Why? How?

Step 2  *Call to act ('main course')*
(a)  **I want you to . . .**
What are your listeners, the contractor, the negotiating partner, the audience to do?
(b)  **I can do . . . for you**
What can you do for your boss, colleague or client?

This is the most important part of your presentation. Find out what you really want. What can you offer? What do you want the other person to do? Say it! Be concrete and specific. Do not beat about the bush. Do not make vague allusions in the hope the other person is a mind-reader:

– Make it clear why this matter is important. You cannot assume that your listeners or partners will understand what you mean straight away. Thoughts that are old hat to you may be quite new to others. Be patient. Help them to understand.
– Check that the other person has understood correctly. There is plenty of room for misunderstanding:

– One and the same word can mean completely different things to different people.

- Perhaps the other person is preoccupied with other things and has not listened properly.
- You have not expressed yourself clearly.

- Be enthusiastic. Show your enthusiasm, and make it clear that you believe in what you are saying. Do not allow yourself to be put off by someone else's ill temper, scepticism or indifference. If you really stand by what you say, sooner or later your positive attitude will catch the imagination of your opposite number.

Step 3   *Advantages and positive results ('Dessert')*
Explain the advantages or positive results the other person can expect if he does as you say, or 'buys' your ideas or products.

Motivate people positively, and 'sell' positive arguments rather than threaten people with negative consequences: 'If you don't do . . . then . . .'. Praise and encourage your listeners or clients.

Your last sentence will be the one which is remembered best. If you have a couple of benefits for the other person, mention the most important in the end of your presentation. For example:

*Sequence of presentation*
(1)   Advantage no. 2 (second important argument).
(2)   Advantage no. 3.
(3)   Advantage no. 4.
(4)   Advantage no. 1 (most important argument).

Remember: whether a customer does finally buy your products or services is not merely a question of quality or price, but also whether he likes you as a person!

There are many irrational moments in the course of the sales process. Build up good relations with everybody whose support you might need at some stage. Bush telephones function both on official occasions and at social gatherings. It is not worth making enemies!

# Exercise 4   Active listening

**Goals**

133  Active listening helps you to be sure you have understood your

partner's point of view correctly. It is one way of avoiding misunderstandings.

**Possible snags**

You are so convinced of being a good listener that you don't care to test your qualities as a conversationalist. Do the exercise anyway, and feel physically what concentrated listening requires.

Active listening techniques were developed by Thomas Gordon, and are described in his book *Leader Effectiveness Training* (LET). They involve repeating in your own words what your partner has said before expressing your own opinion. I developed the following exercise on this basis.

**Application fields**

Active listening techniques can be applied in the situations outlined below.

*Delegation*   If you are delegating something to someone else you can ask the person concerned to repeat what he is supposed to do in his own words. In this way you can avoid later disappointments. For example, 'I want to be sure that I have expressed myself clearly. Would you kindly tell me what message you got?'

*Employee evaluation*   Let the employee summarize the results of his own evaluation, and write a report. Check whether he has got everything right. Even small deviations can have major consequences. If he has left out something completely, ask why. The form of presentation will tell you a lot about his attitude to work, and might be the point of departure for a further discussion.

*Contact with clients*   Clients frequently do not know exactly what they want and, if they do, they often have difficulty in expressing themselves clearly. Be understanding and repeat what has been said: 'If I understand you correctly then . . .' The client now has the opportunity to confirm or rectify your claim: 'No, that's not exactly what I meant. What I really wanted to say was . . .' By using active listening techniques you help your client to clarify his own thoughts.

*Chairing meetings*   When you are in charge of a meeting, summarize how far the discussion has got. This is especially important when there are differences of opinion. Perhaps the participants are agreed on seven of the ten points under discussion, but are arguing bitterly about the last three. The meeting comes to an end, and everyone leaves feeling totally dissatisfied. They are taken up with the three controversial points, and forget that they have actually managed to come to an agreement on the seven others.

Use active listening for your summary: 'If I understand correctly we have come to an agreement on points 1–7.' Everyone nods. 'On the other hand, we still have to agree on solving problems 8, 9 and 10.' By differentiating between the points upon which agreement has been reached and those which still require further discussion, potential conflicts can be kept under control.

## Group exercises for learning active listening techniques

*A word to the trainer*   Make sure the participants are really active and do not use the groupwork as an opportunity to confirm how 'artificial' the exercise is. It is my experience that everyone who really plays by the rules learns a great deal.

*Rules*
- Choose a subject in which everybody is genuinely interested or suggest a topical issue. For example:

  'Should we continue to keep our borders open for refugees and asylum seekers?'
  'During organizational development, should the most able or the least qualified be transferred to another department or a different town?'
  'What are the most important criteria for promoting a member of staff to a post of responsibility (knowledge of the field, length of service, personal characteristics, etc)?'
  'Is the quota-system in women's interest?'
  'Is it true that female staff prefer a male manager?'
  'What sacrifices are you prepared to make to protect the environment?'
  'Should important state contracts be given to native companies on principle, or to the lowest bidder on the world market?'

- Get into groups of three. Two people talk to each other while the third observes them. The exercise lasts about half an hour. Change roles after a while so that everyone has an equal chance to be active and to observe.
- The first person opens the discussion by making a claim. The second person listens carefully and repeats as precisely as possible the claim the first person has made. The first person confirms or corrects what has been repeated.
- The second person continues the discussion by making his own claim. The first person listens carefully and repeats as

precisely as possible the claim the second person has made. The second person confirms or corrects what has been repeated.
- The first person continues the discussion by elaborating his own claim, etc.
- The role of the observer is to check whether the partners have listened, understood, and repeated what has been said correctly. The observer must be very strict.
- Continue this exercise for at least a quarter of an hour. It gets more and more difficult the longer it lasts and particularly when the participants are expressing contradictory opinions. Change roles and let the observer participate in the discussion. Subsequently discuss the observations made.

**Aspirations and reality**

An alternative to this exercise is a role play in which you present, for example, a sales situation. Ask who is a good listener? Get the person who thinks he is to negotiate with a client. Take a video of the scene and then use the film to discuss the person's abilities as a listener. Freezing a particularly characteristic pose can make an enormous impression, and is often more eloquent than words.

## Exercise 5 | Making clear-cut demands

### Goals
This exercise is intended to help you enforce your demands. It is your right and duty as a manager to make clear-cut demands on your staff. As a customer you do not need to accept poor service or sub-quality goods.

If you have complaints or claims to make you will achieve more if you not only grumble but actually tell your staff, business partners or friends quite clearly what you expect of them – and then stick to your demands even when others raise objections.

### Possible snags
When doing this exercise for the first time it may well seem rather artificial. This is a very natural reaction to new and unknown phenomena. Once you have practised assertiveness training a few times you will find yourself using it automatically without even having to think about it first.

This argument technique was developed by the American psychologist Manuel J. Smith, and is described in his book *When I*

*Say No, I Feel Guilty*. The following exercise is however based on my own experience.

## A word to the trainer

Experience shows that at the beginning many people have difficulty, when necessary, in repeating their own claims or demands. They are afraid of making a fool of themselves or being a nuisance. Motivate them to give it at least a try.

Tell them: every time you repeat your point of view you will become more certain of yourself, and the person you are talking to will understand that you really mean it seriously. Perseverance is often the key to success. Think of advertising or politics. How often do they repeat their claims before they are understood and accepted!

## Rules

This technique comprises three elements:

(1) Expressing a wish, making a demand or saying 'no' without feeling guilty.
(2) Active Listening (cf. exercise 4). Letting the person you are talking to know that you are listening carefully to him by repeating in your own words what he has said.
(3) Keep repeating your demand (wish, 'no') until you have achieved your objective or reached a compromise.

   – *I want*   Consider carefully what you really want, and tell the other person exactly and concisely. Be concrete and do not beat about the bush.
   – *Objection*   Be prepared for the person you are addressing to come up with objections.
   – *Active listening*   Show that you respect the person you are addressing by not interrupting him excitedly, but listening to him quietly. Prove that you have understood by repeating what he has said in your own words.
   – *I want*   Follow this by repeating your own point of view. Do not give in. State quite clearly what you expect of the other person.
   – *New objection*   The person you are talking to has other objections at his finger tips explaining why it cannot be done as you wish.
   – *Active listening*   Keep cool and listen to these objections,

**137**

too. Use active listening techniques as proof that you have understood.
- *I want*   Follow this up by stubbonly repeating your own demand. Perseverance will be rewarded, etc., etc., etc.
- *Compromise*   The matter is more complicated than you had thought. Try to meet the person you are talking to half-way and reach a compromise.
- *Higher authority*   The person you are addressing is not prepared to listen, or does not have sufficient authority to make a decision. Move on to a higher authority. Demand to see his superior.
- *Consequences*   You are getting nowhere, the other person is immovable. Threaten him with counter-measures. Indicate the consequences of his behaviour. Even in the heat of battle, however, do not make empty threats you are unable or unwilling to carry out.

**Example of a discussion**

This real-life example features a dialogue between the proprietor of a small firm in an office-service centre and the management of the centre:

*Proprietor*:   Sometimes the phone rings anything up to 12 times before anyone answers. Could you please make sure that there is always someone at the telephone exchange.

*Manager*:   This office-service centre has been in operation since 1981 and there have never been any complaints before.

*Proprietor*:   I know that this office-service centre has been in operation since 1981, and trust you when you say that you have never heard any complaints before. But my clients have actually complained to me that it takes ages before anyone answers. Therefore I insist that the telephones should be answered, and the calls put through more quickly.

*Manager*:   There are such things as difficult clients.

*Proprietor*:   Indeed there are. Clients can be difficult, but in my job I am absolutely reliant on the telephone, and so I want it to be answered more quickly in future.

*Manager*:   Your job's pretty specialized.

*Proprietor*:   I realize you think my work's out of the ordinary. I run open seminars amongst other things, and some of the participants enrol by phone. I really do want a better telephone service.

| | |
|---|---|
| *Manager*: | I can ask the other firms whether they've had complaints, too. |
| *Proprietor*: | I think it is a good idea to ask the other firms whether they've also received complaints. But no matter what their answer is, for my part, I'm sticking to my demand that you get a more modern system, and ensure that there are enough people to staff it even during peak times. |

# Exercise 6

# Questions

**Goals**

The objective of this exercise is to help you to get your audience actively involved in what you are saying by asking them questions.

**Possible snags**

When you are selling a product or service, or giving a speech, and do the talking all alone, there is a danger that the thoughts of your listeners will soon drift away to their own matters of interest. On the other hand, if you ask too many questions at the same time they might feel like they're sitting in a police interrogation. Therefore, find a balance between you and them talking.

When asking a question, give your audience time to think. Don't be afraid of silence. A pause which seems to you to last at least two hours is probably only of 30 seconds.

To engage your audience you can choose between many types of questions:

- Information questions.
- Provocative questions.
- Leading questions.
- Alternative questions.
- Question in reply to a question.

**Information questions**

The objective of information questions is to start a dialogue, or get an overview over existing demands, and trigger exhaustive answers. Information questions start with:

When?
Where?

How?
Whom?
Which?
What?
Why?

## Provocative questions

The purpose of provocative questions is to raise the energy level
in a dull audience, or to heat up a conversation which is in danger
of grinding to a halt. Be careful: by provoking your audience you
may start an emotional process which can easily get out of control.
For example:

- A participant at your seminar is annoying you by chattering
  with his neighbours, always coming in late, frequently leav-
  ing the lecture to take a call, making sarcastic comments,
  etc. You might ask 'I've got the impression that what I say
  is of no interest to you. So why do you waste your time here.
  Why don't you go home?'
- Your company is well behind budget. You call in a meeting
  and ask 'Nobody is interested in making money here?'
- The day after a company party your audience arrives late
  and is hardly listening. You might provoke them by asking
  'Shall we take a sleeping break?'

## Leading questions

The purpose of leading questions is to get the answer you want.
Either the answer already lies in your own question, or you
formulate the question in a way which makes it impossible to
disagree. This might be important in sales situations, or whenever
you want to convince other people. For example:

- Don't you agree . . .?
- Isn't it true . . .?
- Wouldn't it be wonderful if . . .?

Another variant is questions which only can be answered by 'yes'.
This type of question is often used in sales situations. From the
very start of the meeting or telephone call the customer is
stimulated to answer with 'yes' in the hope of also saying 'yes'
when it comes to signing on the dotted line. For example:

- You ring up a prospect and ask 'Am I talking to Mr Smith?'
  Since you dialled his number and he answered with his

**140**

name, you of course know that you are talking with Mr. Smith.
- It's a lovely summer's day and you enter the office of your client: 'Isn't it a wonderful day today?'
- It's a stormy winter's day and your client enters your office: 'Isn't it good to come into a warm place on such a cold winter's day?'

**Alternative questions**

The purpose of alternative questions is to obtain what you want by giving your counterpart two alternatives, both of which are acceptable for you. For example:

- The seller asks the client 'Do you prefer xyz product in red or in blue?' Between the lines he suggests 'You are buying my product.'
- Two teenagers are having a date. Afterwards the boy asks 'Shall we go to my place or to yours?'

**Question in reply to a question**

The purpose of a question in reply to a question is to win time before answering, the better to understand the other person's thoughts and attitudes, or to distract someone's attention from something you don't want to talk about. For example:

- You get a question which you don't know how to answer. You can win time by asking for clarification: 'What do you mean by . . .?', or 'What exactly do you want me to focus on?'
- Your client seems to like your product or service but not its price. You may ask him 'What do you mean by "too expensive"?', or 'Too expensive in relation to what?', or 'What do you compare the price with?'

**Exercise 7** | **Praising and supporting each other**

**Goals**

141 | The goal of this exercise is to increase self-confidence.

**Possible snags**

The praise must be genuine and honest. Ironic comments are hurtful. Exaggeration is not convincing.

This is an exercise for 5–40 people:

- Each one of you holds a two-minute lecture on any subject of your choice. Come forward one after another and speak.
- Concurrently the listeners write positive – and I mean exclusively positive – comments about the person, his or her presentation, or any other aspect on a piece of paper.
- Collect the pieces of paper, put them in an envelope with the name of the lecturer on the outside, and give it to them at the end of the session. Don't open the 'magic box' until you are alone. Don't compare the contents with other participants or discuss the comments you have received.

For most people it is an extraordinary experience to open this envelope. It sensitizes them to positive sides of themselves they were unaware of, especially when several people have made the same comments quite independently of one another.

I know people who have kept their lucky envelope for years and taken it out to comfort themselves when they were feeling depressed.

## Exercise 8 | Giving and accepting positive feedback

**Goals**

The aim of this exercise is to strengthen teamwork by creating trust and generosity.

**Possible snags**

The person getting positive feedback might feel overwhelmed and start crying. This especially happens to women, and is perfectly alright. Provide some paper handkerchiefs and a glass of water just in case. Don't allow the person getting the appreciation to belittle herself, and thereby the person passing on the feedback.

This exercise can be found in the book *Teamwork*! by Barbara Sher and Annie Gottlieb. Here are the instructions:

- Bring your chairs into a close circle.
- Have one person turn his back so he can't see the others,

but can hear them. The turned chair is often called the 'hot seat'. He should have a pencil and paper ready.

- The first person to turn his back should be the most outspoken or extravert. Finding his assets will be easy, and talking to each other about him subtly reveals everyone elses's character. After that the order doesn't matter.
- For about two or three minutes, the rest of you will talk to each other – not to the subject – about his good qualities, as best you can. (In a group where people know each other well I recommend that every single participant gives positive feedback directly to the person on the hot seat and addresses him with his name: 'John, I appreciate . . .').
- When you're finished talking about him, go to the next team member, and so on, until everyone has heard him- or herself praised.
- Describe assets only. No constructive criticism.
- Be specific.

The rules for the subject in the hot seat:

- Write everything down, as dutifully as a secretary taking dictation. Write legibly. You will be surprised how valuable that piece of paper will be to you.
- Don't respond to what you hear. Remember, you're over-hearing people discuss you. Just sit there and take it.
- Use sign language communication if you can't hear clearly what's being said (cup your hand to your ear for 'louder', wave your hand for 'slower').

| Exercise 9 | Unfair criticism |

**Goals**
The objective with this exercise is to make you think three times before you criticize another person. Nobody likes to be criticized. Therefore, it is important that you yourself get more insight in how you react to unfair criticism. If you become clear about your own emotional responses you should be able to develop a more understanding and accepting attitude towards other people, and pause before taking out your own anger on innocent third parties.
**Possible snags**
You don't learn anything if you are not honest with yourself.

**143**  You can do this exercise alone or with a group.

**Individual**

Remember the last time you were criticized. Write down your feelings and compare the result with the common reactions given below.

**Group exercise**

Go into groups of 3–6 people, and share with each other how you react to unfair criticism. Discuss what exactly makes you upset (disappointment about the person giving criticism, emerging self-pity, feeling of guilt, feeling misunderstood, etc.), and how the criticism could have been presented in a more constructive way.

Compare your findings with the following: Answers to the question 'How do you react to unfair criticism?' usually fall into three categories:

- Flight.
- Attack.
- Physical compensation.

*Flight* Flight reactions are taking the criticism to heart and withdrawing depressed. For example: I feel rejected, insecure, worthless, uninspired, discouraged, devastated, frustrated, stupid, bitter, depressed, disappointed, hurt, misunderstood, paralysed, powerless, restricted, totally insignificant, vanquished, unloved.

*Attack* Some people react to criticism with a counter-attack. For example: I'll show the blighter, I am getting aggressive, livid, annoyed, attack, hate, think of revenge, exaggerate and get a negative attitude both to the person and the topic.

*Physical compensation* Some people react to criticism with physical compensation. For example: I bang my fist against the wall, do the washing-up, clean the house, go for a run, have a drink.

## Exercise 10 | Making and taking criticism

**Goals**
The aim of this exercise is to help you criticize others constructively, and to accept their criticism of you self-confidently.

**Possible snags**

The success of this exercise depends on whether you have managed to create a relaxed and informal atmosphere. Since sensitive personal matters might arise, come to an agreement with each other: 'Everything which goes on here will remain our secret.'

- Sit in a circle, preferably without a table.
- Ask the participants when they were last criticized, and considered the criticism unjust and hurtful. Note this criticism on paper. You can decide for yourself whether you want to select an example from work, home, your leisure activities, etc. Make sure that you only note down experiences you are prepared to share with the others.
- Place the papers face-down in a pile in the middle of the circle. Take one each. (If you get your own paper you replace it and take another.)
- Anyone can begin. He or she reads the paper aloud. The 'owner' of the problem identifies himself and fills in background information on the situation in which the criticism was made, and why he felt hurt. There are now two possible ways of continuing:

*Making criticism*  The person who has received another's paper now attempts to reformulate the essence of the criticism so that it becomes constructive (encouragement, I-messages, etc). The other members of the group can also make suggestions. The object of the exercise is for everyone to realize that it is quite legitimate for you to express your misgivings, but the choice of words is decisive.

The recipient listens to the constructively formulated criticism and says whether it would have been easier for him to cope with it if it had been formulated in this way in the actual situation concerned.

*Taking criticism*  The person being criticized tells the others how he reacted to the unjust criticism at the time, and makes suggestions as to how he might have reacted and what he will say in future.

# Exercise 11

# Tackling differences of opinion

**Goals**

The aim of this exercise is to help you to tackle differences of opinion. The best method for solving problems is to anticipate what might happen, and then prevent it from happening, or in advance to agree on the rules on how to solve the problem if it can't be prevented.

Since you can't prevent differences of opinion, decide in advance how to tackle them.

**Possible snags**

You are so afraid of conflicts that you do not allow any differences of opinion to occur in the first place. The boss is always right. Be careful: You might cheat yourself. Problems might pile up, and sooner or later result in an uncontrolled explosion of negative feelings.

There is nothing wrong with differences of opinion. On the contrary, if you manage to harness them in a constructive and creative way, they can lead to new and better solutions. To make it acceptable to talk about unpleasant issues, don't wait until the problems arise, but agree rules on how to tackle differences of opinion in advance. You can choose between different options:

- The manager decides on his own.
- Postpone the decision.
- Come to a compromise.
- Vote.
- Weigh up the advantages and the disadvantages.

**The manager decides on his own**

The senior person takes the decision on his own authority. This is the hierarchical model. The advantage is that decisions can be reached very quickly. The disadvantage, however, is that everyone else probably feels they have been ignored, and starts to plot secret revenge.

**Come to a compromise**

Coming to a compromise means that everyone gives way a little so as to meet the others half-way. The advantage of a compromise is that each person feels they are both giving and taking. The disadvantage, however, may be that at the end of the day no-one is really satisfied with the result. In certain circumstances a bad solution is chosen for the sake of peace. The conflicts are merely postponed.

**Vote**

If it is not possible to come to an agreement any other way, the participants can vote by raising their hands or by secret ballot. The advantage of this is that it is a democratic solution, respected by all. However, the disadvantage of this procedure is that it creates winners and losers. Nobody likes being a loser. When the vote is close, there is a particular danger that the losing side will build up a store of negative feeling, retreat apathetically, or declare open warfare.

### Weigh up the advantages and the disadvantages

When there are differences of opinion it doesn't usually take long before it becomes a question of prestige, who is right and who is wrong. Everyone is afraid of losing face, and thus fights bitterly for their own point of view even though, secretly, they may be haunted by initial doubts. Giving in equals weakness.

In such intractable situations it is usually the person in the highest position within the company, or the one with the best rhetorical abilities, who wins in the end. But this is not always the person who has come up with the best solution.

Instead of fighting bitterly the participants can quietly weigh up the advantages and disadvantages of the respective suggestions, and then come to a decision. With the benefit of newly-gained insights it is then possible to take leave of dearly-loved opinions without forfeiting one's honour (cf. exercise 12).

## Exercise 12 | Modifying entrenched positions solving conflicts (PMI-method)

### Goals
The PMI-method can help you to temper entrenched positions and solve conflicts.

### Possible snags
Lack of willingness to solve the problem. If you are so negative that you cannot even be bothered to look at things from various points of view, this method is of no use whatsoever. So pull yourself together, and try a positive attitude to life.

The PMI-method (P = plus, M = minus, I = interesting) was developed by Edward de Bono, and can be found in his book *Conflicts*. The following summary is my own work.

In a conflict the following might occur:

**147** It is frequently a question of power (title, position, rhetoric skills) as to who wins a battle, and not of quality (what is in the best interests of the matter at hand).

The more aggressive the attacker becomes, the more bitterly the loser will defend his point of view. Both become more and more intractable. Neither of them will try to develop new ideas. They are preoccupied with winning or losing. Both waste a great deal of time and energy pursuing this unproductive argument. The creativity of those involved is not channelled into finding improvements, but only into dealing the opponent a deadly blow. In the end, the strongest gets his idea through, but it is not necessarily the best idea.

To escape from this trap, Edward de Bono suggests using the PMI-method to investigate the ideas first, i.e. to look at the matter from various angles instead of dismissing it without due consideration. This procedure has the following advantages:

- Nobody starts attacking an old idea. If those involved are really unable to come up with anything better it can be rehabilitated without anyone having to lose face.
- Everyone thinks creatively from the start. Valuable time is not wasted in useless arguments, but is channelled into positive thought.
- As it is not the object of the exercise to bring something into disrepute, it might be possible to improve on an already good idea. The atmosphere is right for useful cooperation.
- Nobody has a monopoly on good ideas ('your' idea is lousy, 'my' idea is brilliant).

**Rules for the PMI-method**

- Begin with a brainstorming session dealing with all the positive aspects of the matter. Write down the results on a flipchart, and hang the pages up on the wall.
- Then list all the negative aspects and hang them up.
- In the third round, write down everything which is interesting without actually being negative or positive.

My personal experiences with the PMI-method have been very good in relation to the following problem areas:

- What are the advantages and disadvantages of a specific suggestion?
- What are the criteria by which we should decide on promoting staff (length of service/competence/communication skills)?

**148**

- How should we evaluate what has happened? What can we learn from it?
- What are the criteria by which we should determine who is supposed to work in which project group?
- What are the criteria by which we should decide on job-assignment to individual departments?

# Exercise 13 | Seeing the opposite point of view

**Goals**

This exercise is designed to help you to solve conflicts by looking at the issue from your opponent's point of view. By being forced to present his case correctly you can avoid misunderstandings due to misinterpretation and obtain an understanding of his attitude.

**Possible snags**

If you lack willingness to reach a mutual agreement, no communication technique whatsoever can solve the matter. Then the outcome of the conflict is solely a question of power. However, keep in mind that you can win a battle and lose the war. It might very well be in your own interests to pull yourself together, show self-discipline, and work on a solution which all parties involved can accept.

**A word to the trainer**

Create a positive working atmosphere. Show the opponents the benefits of reaching an agreement. Some people might argue that this exercise is 'artificial'. This is usually a 'left-brain argument' for hiding a 'right-brain feeling': 'I am afraid of making a fool of myself. I am afraid of losing control. I am afraid of giving in and thus being looked at as a weak person.' Therefore, build up mutual trust, motivate the participants to engage in the role play, but never actually force them to do something they don't feel comfortable with.

This exercise is a role play which can be carried out in two different ways.

*Discussion with two people* Two people talk to each other about a problem for which they each have a different solution. Person A has to present Person B's point of view to the latter's full satisfaction, and vice versa.

*Group discussion*   A project group, which is unable to agree on a matter, divides its members into two groups. Group A is automatically in favour, and lists the positive aspects of a suggestion. Group B is against and only presents the negative aspects.

# Exercise 14

# See yourself in the mirror

### Goals
The aim of this exercise is to help you to get to know yourself better. If you become aware of your weak points this is the first step along the road towards mastering difficult situations better.
### Possible snags
This exercise is useless if you are not honest with yourself. You have to face up to yourself and confront your bad points.

This exercise is inspired by Anne Dickson's book *A Woman in Your Own Right – Assertiveness and You*, though the following description is my own.

Step 1   *Difficult situation*
Make a list of situations you would like to be able better to deal with: at work, at home, with friends, with people in authority, etc.

Step 2   *Order of precedence*
Arrange the situations according to their degree of difficulty. No. 1 is the easiest, No. 10 the most difficult problem. Draw up a strategy of how you want to behave in future. Remember: self-confidence has to be built up slowly. Begin with the easiest things and work your way gradually down the list.

Step 3   *A common pattern*
Get to the heart of the matter. The situation may differ considerably, but your reactions are the same. Can you recognize a common pattern? What makes you absolutely livid? Someone doubting your qualifications or your intentions? Do you feel guilty because you think someone else has a right to something you are not prepared to give them? Why can't you be quiet and objective when criticized? Are you really angry with the person criticizing you, or is it that they remind you of aspects of yourself you would prefer to forget?

Step 4    *Positive affirmations*

Use creative visualization and positive affirmations (cf. exercise 16) to build up confidence that you can change your attitudes and reaction patterns.

The better you know yourself, the easier it will be to think up a strategy for mastering difficult situations in future. Be patient with yourself. A change in behaviour can take years. Today is the first day of the rest of your life.

Let yourself make mistakes and suffer setbacks. When we set out along new paths we are always in danger of slipping and falling over. If we lay down on our stomachs we are fairly secure, but do not actually make a great deal of progress.

# 2 | Visions, goals and strategy

In this section you will find exercises relating to Part I of this book, *Motivation and Organizational Transformation*.

Clear goals are a prerequisite for managing organizational change. Of course, we never know exactly in advance which challenges we are going to face. But by creating shared visions, stimulating our intuition and giving room for fantasy and creativity, we become more aware of our own role in the process of transformation. Instead of awaiting passively what might happen to us, we can choose to play an active part in forming the future.

Clear goals are also an important motivation factor. The very best working atmosphere will soon be spoiled if the employees don't know what they are supposed to do, and why. A shared vision and open communication are two sides of the same coin.

# Personal and company purpose

**Goals**

The aim of this exercise is to help the organization find its purpose and a vision everybody can identify with.

**Possible snags**

Companies which define their main purpose as 'making profit' are in danger of adopting policies that are not in their own interest in the long run. (For example: too little concern with environmental issues might drive customers and employees away; too much focus on short-term profits might result in lack of research and development, incorrect investment decisions and high turnover of qualified personnel, etc.).

Profit is not a goal in itself, but a by-product of doing the right things in the right way. So the real challenge for the company is to find 'What is our deeper purpose? How can we motivate staff to realize our vision?'

This exercise is inspired by Sabrina Spencer and John Adam's book *Life Changes*. It is a combination of personal and organizational development. First, every employee works on his own purpose individually, then they form groups so as to create a shared purpose for the company.

## 1 Individual purpose

*Preparation* Write the success story of your own life. Imagine that someone intends to make a film based on your life. Write a brief giving the actor detailed information on the main person in the film. Write about yourself as 'he' or 'she':

- What did he/she do which made him/her successful?
- What are his/her assets?
- What kind of human being is he/she?
- Which accomplishments has he/she achieved?
- etc.

You can focus on private life, job situations or personal hobbies. Don't be modest. Nobody else is going to read what you write. Now is the time for praising the genius you are.

*Personal mastery*

Step 1  *Personal assets*
Look at your success story once more, and list at least

three positive characteristics of yourself as a human being (for example, open, good communicator, enthusiastic, fair, etc).

Step 2    *Professional assets*
Look at your success story once more and list at least three professional strong points (for example, knowledge, competence, intellectual abilities, creativity, etc).

Step 3    *A meaningful life*
How can you use steps 1 and 2 to give your life more meaning? Imagine that you are 99 years old and there is not too much time left. You are looking back on your life, and say to yourself 'It was good and meaningful. Perhaps not everything turned out as I wished, but I did what I could for living the life I wanted. Sometimes it was painful, but I tried to learn from my mistakes. Sometimes I had no influence on what happened in my surroundings, but I worked on my own response to external factors. I took responsibility for my own well-being, and did not look for scapegoats when something went wrong. I knew what I wanted and I grasped opportunities when they turned up. I chose the right balance between being a professional and reserving enough time to my family and friends. All in all it has been a fulfilled life.'

Take a fundamental decision now: 'What is my purpose? What changes do I need for living a meaningful life? Which sacrifices am I willing to do to obtain the right balance between job, private life and work for the global survival?

Take a relaxation exercise, and try to visualize (cf. exercise 16) that you reach your goal. See, hear and feel what it really means to live a meaningful life.

Step 4    *Need for professional and personal development*
Be honest with yourself: what need do you have for professional training and personal development so as to reach your goal? Take the fundamental decision now that you are willing to learn.

Step 5    *Revised purpose*
Trust in yourself that you can develop yourself both as a human being and as a professional. You are willing to learn and to adjust. You can get it if you really want. What is your real purpose?

**155**

## 2 Company purpose

Go into groups of 5–9 people and choose a group leader. The facilitator writes on a flipchart and participates actively in the work:

Step 1   *Personal assets in the company*
Share with the other group members one of your positive characteristics as a human being. Write the various strong points on a flipchart and hang it on the wall.

Step 2   *Professional assets in the company*
Share with each other one professional strength, write the various skills on a flipchart, and hang it on the wall.

Step 3   *Individual drafts for company purpose*
Individual work: taking into account the company's available resources (cf. steps 1 and 2), make a suggestion for the company's purpose, write it on half a flipchart and hang it on the wall.

Step 4   *Agree on a common purpose*
Look at the various drafts and coordinate them to one single sentence. For example:

- Enthusiasm and knowledge are the source of development.
- We strengthen our self-confidence to release creative energy so that we can live in harmony with ourselves, our family and the company.
- We use willpower and teamwork to support each other so that we can meet new challenges and create an economically sound company where it is fun to work.
- We support teamwork and creativity, and motivate our employees to develop their human and professional skills so that the company is able to manage future challenges.
- We motivate employees to lifelong learning by allowing the individual to take their own initiatives and decisions so that everybody experiences the company as a postive place to work. This results in happy customers and a safe municipality.
- We motivate women to be clear about their goals so that they can actively participate in the restructuring of the company.

**156**

# Exercise 16 | Creative visualization

**Goals**

Creative visualization is a powerful technique to clarify your goals, and strengthen your belief that you can achieve your goals if you really want to.

A welcome by-product is stress management. When you contemplate your goal in a peaceful state of mind, you mobilize the necessary energy to be perseverant and tackle creative tension.

In addition, you will improve your concentration skills.

**Possible snags**

To be effective it is not enough to do the exercise once in a while. You need self-discipline, and should practise every day – yes, every single day – even if it is only two minutes a few times, or once for 15–20 minutes, depending on the kind of relaxation method you use to achieve your Alpha-state.

Creative visualization can be used both individually to reach personal goals, and in a group for revealing company aims. Instead of only thinking analytically with your left-brain you also use your imagination, fantasy and subconscious mind to help achieve your objectives by creating mental pictures of a desired outcome. When you face a challenge your subconscious is already programmed to trust that you can, want and dare to succeed. The chances of actually achieving something are much greater than when you keep telling yourself you can't do it.

You can achieve a vision as follows:

Step 1   *Setting your goals*

Use your head to formulate a goal worth fighting for (for example, your relationship with your boss, colleagues, clients, family, friends). Collate facts, hopes, dreams, dangers and possibilities, and write on a piece of paper what you would like to achieve in as much detail as possible.

A desired outcome can be described with the help of both the mind and the senses:

mind:    Figures, deadlines, etc.
senses:   What do you want to *see* happen?
             What will you *feel* when it happens?
             What will you *hear* when it has happened?

Check whether you can identify with this goal and are keen to achieve it. Is it something you yourself want, or something you think others are expecting of you? Would you really take it if you could get it?

Step 2    *Relaxation and creative visualization*
Sit down with your back straight, or lie down in a relaxed position on the floor. Breathe deeply and regularly from your diaphragm. There are many ways to get into an Alpha-state. Relaxation exercises are difficult to learn from a book alone. I therefore recommend you take a class in one of the following techniques:

- autogen training.
- progressive relaxation.
- self-hypnosis.
- meditation.
- Silva-mind control.

If you are not acquainted with these techniques, just concentrate on your breathing (exhale; pull in the stomach muscles; inhale; release the stomach muscles). Close your eyes and abandon yourself to the feeling of relaxing. Do not fight against disturbing thoughts. Let them come and go. If there is still any place in your body where you feel tension, bring your attention to where the tension is, and imagine that you can breathe in and out through this part of your body.

When you are perfectly relaxed you can start to paint mental images of your vision. Allow yourself to rely on your intuition.

Go on a mental journey from the present situation to the point when the goal has been realized. Imagine, for example, that this has taken one, three or five years and you are looking back to the present. Use imagination to create a picture ('see'). What is different? What have been the consequences for whom? What do those involved think about it? Try to 'hear' what they say. What does this mean to you? Think about how it 'feels' to have achieved your goal, and why it is good to be there, or what you would have to do differently to get it right. Which of your own and your colleagues' emotional needs have been satisfied? If you can find something to 'smell' or to 'taste', all the better. The point is to mobilize all the senses.

You have to be convinced that you can achieve your goal (experience the breakthrough of your ideas at a meeting, carry through a successful campaign, win new

**158**

clients or overcome your fear of authority). Be realistic, but optimistic.

Come back to a normal waking state and write down any insights you might have obtained.

In addition to creative visualization you might also paint your goal with your left hand. Drawing often gives new insights. Things you thought were really important to you don't appear at all in your painting. So perhaps they are not that important as you always thought. Or vice versa: you suddenly find yourself painting things you were not aware of before.

*Group exercise:* Share your new insights with your colleagues. Piece together all the various visions to create a joint vision for the company as a whole. The more this vision attains a balance between hard and soft values, the more attractive it will become. An employee who feels his own needs are being recognized will fall over backwards to achieve the company's overriding objective (cf. exercise 15).

Step 3    *Overcoming mental barriers*
Now look at all obstacles which might come into your way. Examine both external challenges and your own mental barriers. Who or what is actually stopping you reaching your goal?

*External factors*

- Who is preventing you from getting what you want? What do they say? How are they treating you? What threats do they make? What is your own response to their attitudes and actions?
- What is the worst that could possibly happen? What is the likelihood that it will happen? What will happen when it happens? What expedients are there? Will you be able to survive?

*Mental barriers*
Write down all negative thoughts about yourself:

- What negative thoughts do you have about yourself? (For example: 'I'll never get it. I don't deserve it. Nobody appreciates what I am doing anyway. I feel underestimated, etc).
- Which arguments do you use – consciously or

**159**

unconsciously – to prevent yourself from doing things you really consider to be important and right?
- Try to get clear about your own patterns of thought. Do you focus on what you want or on what you want to avoid. Do you see reality as it really is or as you expect it to be? Do you look at yourself as a victim or as the biggest creative force in your life? Do you look for a scapegoat if something goes wrong (my husband/wife doesn't understand me, my boss is a lousy leader, it's the bad economic times, the Japanese take it all anyway), or do you accept responsibility for your own personal well-being and professional success?

Step 4  *Positive affirmations*
Have another look at your list of minus points. Now reformulate your negative thoughts to make them positive. Use present tense and avoid norms and negative words like 'must', 'should not', 'ought to'. Plump for 'want' and 'dare'. For example:

- When you are taking a risk you can tell yourself 'I'm really pleased I'm going to be able to do xyz' (and not 'I must do so and so', or 'I mustn't make a mistake on any account').
- When you feel fear of authority you can give yourself the following affirmation: 'I am in the process of enjoying talking to top management', or 'I am in the process of enjoying making telephone calls to very important people' (and not 'I must not tremble or stumble').
- When you are afraid of rejection you can tell yourself 'I am welcome. I am appreciated. I am counted on' (and not 'I hope they don't look down at me').
- When you want to stop drinking: 'I want a clear head and good health and I enjoy mineral water' (and not 'I mustn't drink any alcohol. It's harming my liver').
- When you want to stop smoking: 'I enjoy breathing fresh, clean air' (and not 'I shouldn't smoke any more').

Write down all the positively formulated objectives in the

form of short slogans. Tell them to yourself again and again. When you are alone talk loud to yourself. To programme your subconscious mind positively you have to practise every single day for 5–10 minutes until you yourself accept that you have deserved success. Mind you: when you are getting annoyed at other people it is often your own lack of self-confidence you are annoyed at.

Step 5    *Relaxing and visualizing*
Sit down again with your back straight, or lie down on the floor. Close your eyes. Breathe deeply and regularly. Go to an Alpha-state of mind. When you feel perfectly relaxed call on your imagination to see how you yourself create a lot of obstacles, how you overcome your mental barriers, and how you can achieve your objectives if you really want.

Visualize, i.e. let a film run through your head in which you play the main role. You want to do something, you dare to do something, and you can do it. Look at what happens. Activate all your senses. Relish every moment of achieving your goal.

Step 6    *Revised goals*
Look at your goal one more time and revise it according to the new insights you have gained during the process (cf. steps 1–5). Formulate your goal clearly (cf. exercise 1). Take another visualization or paint your goal once more.

If you train regularly you will discover that situations which used to frighten you no longer do so to the same extent. Your confidence in yourself will grow and lead to success.

I have found this exercise most helpful not only during times of emotional stress, but also in connection with skiing. My favourite cross-country track finishes with a pretty steep descent which suddenly turns left – and just to the right of the bend is a great big birch tree. For years I used to brake just before the descent and always fell just in front of the tree. I did not fall because I was a bad skier who could not negotiate bends, but because I was afraid, already visualizing my leg in plaster, and thus preferred to land securely on my bottom.

I then began to work on my mental barriers. Before every descent I always said to myself 'This is fun. I can do it. I am a good skier.' Since then I have stopped falling.

# Focus and flexibility

## Goals
When the goal is clear and you have found out what you really want (cf. exercises 15 and 16), it is important to *do* something so as to reach your objective. You need both focus and flexibility.

## Possible snags
When you try to do everything at once you are in danger of achieving nothing. Therefore, keep your goal always in mind and learn to say 'no'.

Focused action means:

- Give everything you do your complete and undivided attention.
- Restrict your activities to those you do best or those you might genuinely manage to perfect.
- Concentrate on one thing at a time, i.e. when you are dealing with one thing, cut out everything else.
- Be flexible enough to be able to switch from one activity to another, but when you have started on a new task put the old one out of your mind.
- Believe in what you are doing, and be convinced that it is worthwhile. The more you take an interest in something the easier it becomes to focus your thinking and acting on your objective.
- Be aware of your colleagues' interests. Arouse their interest before suggesting changes. Make clear to everyone the requirements which will be fulfilled by the planned changes. Consider in detail what the consequences of the innovations will be for whom.
- Find yourself supporters who will assist you in your undertaking.
- Be perseverant and do not give in at the first setback.
- As it might take a very long time to see changes through, and you might feel burnt out and exhausted, this would be the time to get in some new blood. Job rotation might prove very effective.
- Once you have learnt to think and act focusing on your goal you can start to cut out activities which do not lead to this goal.

The objective should be clear, but the path leading to the objective has to be flexible. To avoid becoming bogged down in the old ways and patterns of thinking:

- Think about the new ideas and do something about them.
- Follow up your ideas with action.
- Have good relations with the users of your services.
- Take note of what is happening around you.
- Make sure everybody is heading in the same direction.
- Take note of international developments and be aware of how global changes might affect your own working situation.
- Try to predict effects in good time.

# Exercise 18 | Strategy

**Goals**
The aim of this exercise is to help you to develop a strategy for your company.

**Possible snags**
If you approach the matter with a negative attitude your bad mood will rub off onto others. In this sort of atmosphere it is quite impossible to be creative. Listen carefully before dismissing suggestions out of hand: 'That'll never work!'

Start with relaxation exercises, and by visualizing objectives (cf. exercise 16). Then continue with a brainstorming session referring to the following points:

*Target groups*

- Who are our clients?
- Sorting out priorities (cf. exercise 19): who are our most important clients? Paretos' 80:20 rule says that 20% of our customers give us 80% of our profits while the remaining 80% of our clients only account for 20% of our profits. Is this true for us? What are we going to do with it?

*Needs*

- What are our most important clients' needs and requirements?
- Sorting our priorities (cf. exercise 19): what are the most important needs of our clients which we can and want to satisfy?

*Products and services*

**163**     - Which products and services does our company offer?

- To what extent are we satisfying the requirements of our most important clients?
- What is missing? What is superfluous?
- What are the strong and weak sides of our company in relation to the needs of our most important clients?
- What competences do we have?
- What competences do we need?
- What competences should we acquire?
- What competences should we not acquire?

# Exercise 19 | Priorities

### Goals
This exercise is designed to help you to sort out your priorities. When having the vision clear (cf. exercises 15 and 16), or having been through an organizational diagnosis (cf. exercise 25), it is important that you develop a plan of action which tells you what to do when. The exercise can also assist you in taking a decision when faced with various alternatives.

### Possible snags
There may be so many things to do which all seem equally important. If you try to do everything at once you will not manage anything at all. You will be in danger of dissipating your resources.

### A word to the facilitator

Be prepared for previously hidden conflicts of opinion and interest to emerge when you are discussing priorities. After all, we are dealing with power and money.

Thus try to anticipate what will happen, and decide in advance how you are going to deal with conflicts.

Some people like to hear their own voice. They talk and talk. Make sure the discussion does not gradually start going round in circles without producing any new points of view. Use active listening techniques (cf. exercise 4) to summarize and interrupt people politely when they start to repeat themselves.

### Rules for sorting out priorities

The two methods given below should help you to work effectively and creatively.

*'Elephant-Gallup'*

This is an alternative form of voting, where everybody not only 'hears' but also 'sees' the result. The main thing is that nobody has a complete overview of how anyone else is voting. This helps to avoid people acting like a flock of sheep following the leader. The individual feels at greater liberty to express his opinion without having to fear retribution from his boss at a later stage.

Usually the visualized result makes an enormous impression on people:

- Make it clear what the alternatives are, and write them down for everyone to see (flipchart, blackboard, etc).
- Give the participants a few minutes for thought.
- Distribute 'elephants', i.e. the sort of little stickers you can buy in any stationers. (Of course, you can also use other motifs or coloured spots. Funny pictures put people in a good mood.)
- Explain the rules: when you say 'start' everyone rushes at the same time to the flipchart/blackboard and sticks their 'elephant' on the respective spot.
- Read aloud what the result is, and make sure that everyone accepts the majority vote.

*Weighing up one against the other*

Divide the various suggestions into groups of two and weigh up one against the other. For example:

A and B: which suggestion is more important? Which should be disregarded?
C and D: which suggestion is more important? Which should be disregarded?
E and F: and so on.

In the next round you could choose between A and D, etc.

You can also combine this exercise with creative visualization (cf. exercise 16). Go into an Alpha-state, weigh up one against the other, and 'see', 'hear' and 'feel' which solutions you prefer.

**Exercise 20**

# Plan of action

**Goals**

This exercise is designed to help you to draw up a plan of action for achieving your objective.

**Possible snags**

The biggest challenge is self-discipline. Talking is not walking. Do what you have agreed upon.

Your plan of action should answer the following questions:

- On which areas do we want to concentrate in future?
- Who?
- What?
- How?
- When?
- Where?
- Why? (Purpose cf. exercise 15).
- Why not?
- For how long?
- What will make us change direction?

# 3 | Organizational development

The exercises in this section will help you to achieve organizational transformation by participation. It is a collection of methods and guidance for making teamwork function effectively.

**Goal**

The object of this exercise is to emphasize creativity at meetings, in project groups and at seminars by recognizing potential rather than limitations.

**Possible snags**

This exercise requires a good atmosphere where no-one is afraid of making a fool of themselves. The more hierarchical and bureaucratic an organization is, the less imagination the staff tend to show.

This exercise is suited both to warming-up at the beginning of a meeting/seminar, and prior to taking decisions about prioritizing dissimilar tasks or fields of activity.

Appeal to the groups' creativity and say:

- 'Imagine you are a mighty king or queen reigning over a kingdom. You are rich. Money is not a problem. Everything is possible. There are no restrictions. The king or queen makes decisions and what they decide will happen. Use your fantasy. If you were such a king or queen, how would you tackle your own job, a particular problem, a product strategy, etc?'
- Allow one minute for thought, and then pass from one person to the next until everyone has had their say.
- Ask subsequently: 'Who or what actually prevents us from doing precisely what we have said?' Even the most insane ideas can provide the momentum for genuine solutions.

| Exercise | **Noting expectations** |
| 22 | |

**Goals**

The aim of this exercise is to avoid disappointments, misunderstandings and conflicts by anticipating potential problems. Before rushing into a new project take time to note people's expectations and try to arrive at a shared concept of reality.

**Possible snags**

Noting people's expectations should not take the form of an interrogation in which the leader puts the questions and the staff feel it incumbent upon themselves to say something intelligent to impress their boss.

**A word to the facilitator**

At the beginning of a seminar or start of a new project, take a briefing on what participants hope to get out of it. Create a relaxed atmosphere. Especially when people don't know each other, they tend to be insecure and keyed-up. Make them feel comfortable.

Even if you are the boss and thus the one who says what's what in the company, resist the temptation to punish your staff at a later date for things they have said. Otherwise, it will be the first and last time they will ever be honest with you.

If you feel your staff are really on the wrong track, use the opportunity to explain the whys and wherefores to them. Taking this attitude you can even make good use of critical remarks.

**Methods for noting expectations**

*Oral method*   Ask the participants to verbalize their expectations, and give them up to five minutes to think and make notes. Choose one person (but not the boss or most senior person present) to express his expectations. Go round in a clockwise direction so that everyone has a chance to say what he thinks.

*Flipchart*   As above. In addition, write down all the expectations on a flipchart and hang up the pages on the wall. Comment on the points. Channel this round into a discussion about the aims and objectives of the current project or measures, etc.

*Pin-board method*   Hang up ordinary brown packing paper on the wall and treat it with spray-glue. Give each participant several half-sheets of A4 paper cut length-ways and a black felt-tip pen. White down expectations in keywords, and go up together to stick the sheets of paper on the wall. Thus you avoid any suggestion of mutual control. Arrange the material together according to topic. Comment on the points. If you use the same meeting room during the whole seminar/project, let the sheets of paper hang on the wall. Remove them only when the expectations are fulfilled.

# Exercise 23 | Agreeing on the rules

**Goals**

**169** | The objective of this exercise is to avoid conflicts by agreeing on the rules in advance. Cooperation will improve if the participants respect both each other and the jointly-agreed rules.

**Possible snags**

Do not play the schoolmaster (or mistress) teaching your infants the alphabet. The more you threaten them the more rebellious they will become: 'We'll show you . . .' Choose a lighter vein.

The reverse-method described here allows each individual to articulate potential fears right at the beginning of a discussion, seminar, etc. When everything is out in the open the participants can then concentrate on the work in hand, and will not be distracted by niggling doubts previously suppressed.

To anticipate what might go wrong, ask right at the beginning of a meeting or seminar:

- 'What can we do to make this discussion (seminar, project, session, etc.) as unpleasant as possible?'
- 'What could each of you do to ensure that this project is a disaster?'
- 'How can we organize the work to guarantee that you walk out of this room feeling totally frustrated?'
- 'What is the very worst thing that can happen?' etc.

Let each participant make destructive suggestions, note them down on a flipchart, and hang them up on the wall for everyone to see. For example:

- Endless monologues/lectures.
- Boring topics.
- An arrogant group leader.
- An empty discussion – in effect, everything has been decided in advance.
- A troublemaker.
- People cutting each other off in mid-sentence.
- Arriving late.
- Too few or too short breaks.
- Not playing straight.
- Manipulation.
- Stabbing each other in the back.

If someone does not abide by the rules, you indicate the relevant point on the flipchart and say something along the lines of:

'There's a red warning light flashing here. Can you see it?'

'I think we're entering a danger zone. Do you agree?'

At the end of the discussion, evaluate the working atmosphere with reference to the rules agreed on in advance.

## Exercise 24 | Superteams

**Goals**
The aim of this exercise is to help you to make teamwork succeed in practice.
**Possible snags**
The biggest challenge to teamwork is bad planning and jealousy among colleagues. Build up your self-esteem, and learn to appreciate others' success.

In their book *The Superteam Solution: Successful Teamworking in Organizations*, Colin Hastings, Peter Bixby and Rani Chaudhry-Lawton from the Ashridge Management College give advice on how to make teamwork function in practice. The following summary is my own.

Instead of rushing into a new project, give yourself time to anticipate potential problems, note expectations, and agree on the goal and rules for cooperating.

### The team's internal life

*Expectations – criteria for success*
- How shall we judge whether we have achieved our objective?
- Which are the decisive criteria for success?
- Who defines what counts as success?
- The company's top managers? The team leaders? The participants? Others outside the team?
- What does the company expect of the team?
- What does the team expect of the company?
- What does the team expect of the project leader?
- What does the project leader expect of the individual members of the team?
- What do the participants expect of each other?

*Clearly defined goals – planning the 'what'*
- Common vision.
- Objective of the concrete project.
- Definition of tasks.
- Obstacles.
- Economic framework.

- Timetable.
- Working requirements.
- Clarification of responsibility and authority.

*Rules for cooperating – planning the 'how'*
- Working environment.
- Communication.
- Information.
- Efficient meetings.

*Project leadership*
- Role of leader.
- Coordination with environment.

**Relationship to the environment**

*Relationship team – company*
- Project leader – line manager.
- Team – top management.

*Relationship team – environment outside the company*
- Network (support from other companies, research institutions, governmental departments, etc.)
- Image, marketing.
- Resources.

# Exercise 25

# Gaining an organizational overview

**Goals**

This exercise is intended to help you to gain an overview of the current situation within your company or public-service institution. It consists of brainstorming and structuring the material in a team effort.

**Possible snags**

Some people think there are no rules for brainstorming. Personally, I think this is wrong. Brainstorming is 'structured chaos'. In the following a number of rules are indicated.

**Where brainstorming can be applied**

*Organizational diagnosis*   Brainstorming is a method of producing a list of potential improvement points in the organization. Sometimes it is useful to make a diagnosis of the present situation before starting to solve problems. Particularly when managers and staff share their views, they will be able to see reality as it is, and not as they wished it were.

*Marketing*   If you want to try out something new in marketing, or find a fine-sounding name for a new product, it is worth trying out brainstorming.

*Strategy*   Take advantage of people's imagination when searching for a new strategy. You can always change something later. Brainstorming is particularly effective if you precede it with relaxation exercises and visualize the intended objectives (cf. exercise 16). Let yourself be inspired by visions, i.e. think about the potentialities rather than the restrictions.

*Personnel development*   To locate training and in-service require-ments you can distribute a written questionnaire (cf. Appendix), or you can involve your staff in a brainstorming session.
    In the following I focus on brainstorming as a tool for organiza-tional diagnosis. The process described here was inspired by Ichak Adizes' methods. The comments and analysis chart are my own.

*A word to the consultant*   The advantages of an organizational diagnosis are that managers and staff talk to each other – often for the first time. This releases energy. There are, however, two dangers involved:

- The brainstorming of problems might result in a search for a scapegoat. If the participants are not able to communicate with each other, the situation might turn out worse than before. Therefore, it is your task as a consultant to create a relaxed atmosphere, and to teach people how to talk about difficult matters without hurting each other.
- A brainstorming-session of two hours can result in 200–300 potential improvement points. But brainstorming problems is not the same as solving them. People are tempted to expect that a lot of things will change very soon and get disappointed if nothing – or too little – happens. Working on all the problems, however, takes too much time. You cannot close the company while developing the organization.

Before starting the process, talk to the top manager face to face or in private. Inform him on what is going to happen, which methods are going to be used, and what can be the consequences. Tell him not to intervene, even if he disagrees with somebody

173

else's views. And vice versa: never allow a member of the staff to attack the boss. Do your best to create a team spirit.

Also, be aware that people who are getting down to the 'nitty-gritty' often feel a need to unload their frustration on someone else – and that person might very well be you, the consultant. It's all your fault. The worst you can do is starting to defend yourself or going on a counter-attack. Keep calm, and don't let them provoke you.

## Rules for organizational diagnosis

*Individual collating of ideas*   Explain the objectives and rules. Depending on topic and need, allow a period for thought of 1–20 minutes. Note down keywords on a piece of paper. There should be silence during this phase so that everyone can really concentrate on what they are doing.

If this individual compiling of ideas takes more than a quarter of an hour it is worth taking a break afterwards. However, don't discuss the points you have noted with each other.

*Joint collating of ideas*   You have two alternatives:

- Everyone who wants to can say something:

  *Advantage*:      Immense spontaneity.
  *Disadvantage*:   Some participants hog the show, others cannot get a word in. Good suggestions do not get heard.
- Any person (except the boss) starts to speak. Everybody else is listening. The speaker indicates that he has finished by passing the word to his neighbour on his right and addressing him or her by name: 'Over to you, Mr Biggs':

  *Advantage*:      Everybody gets the chance to say something. You don't have to struggle to get attention.
  *Disadvantage*:   When there are more than 20 participants people tend to get restless. It takes too long before they get their turn.

*Rules for brainstorming sessions*
- Preferably 3–20 people. It is possible to work with bigger groups, but this demands a lot of patience and discipline.
- A positive working climate. It's a good idea to start with warming-up exercises. Make people feel relaxed.
- No interruptions.

- Number the suggestions and write them on a flipchart. Ask an assistant to hang them up on the wall. If you are expecting a large number of suggestions it is worth using two flipcharts and having two people writing them down. The first then notes down problems 1,3,5,7, etc., the second 2,4,6,8, etc.
- Be as brief as possible.
- Choose the following formulations:

  We need.
  We lack.
  Too bad.
  Too little (of a good thing).
  Too much (of a bad thing).

- Be as concrete as possible.
- Formulations such as 'poor leadership' are too imprecise. Ask for greater precision: 'What exactly do you mean by "poor"? Too little information about what? Too little participation in what? The boss is not sufficiently approachable – when and for whom? In which department?' (cf. exercise 1).
- List potential improvement points and do not attack people!
- While collating ideas there should be no discussion.
- Don't criticize, throw out suggestions or make them look ridiculous. ('That's not true!', 'Smith's barking up the wrong tree!', 'Did you ever hear anything that stupid?', etc).
- If a participant fails to understand the contents of a statement he is allowed to ask: 'Do you mean . . .' (cf. exercise 4 Active Listening). The person questioned should only answer 'yes' or 'no'. No mammoth explanations!
- No breaks in-between.
- Brainstorming sessions develop their own dynamism. When analysing problems participants usually begin with safe points ('The photocopier is always out of order.'). After half an hour or so someone will take it upon themselves to get down to the nitty-gritty. This is the breakthrough. Now the others will also have the courage to open their mouths.
- A break would interrupt this dynamic process. A burning desire for a break is often just a subconscious attempt to flee when things start hotting up.
- Duration: 20 minutes to 2 hours.

*Sorting and structuring*   To prevent yourself drowning in a sea of problems, it is worth arranging the material according to subject and deciding on priorities. Let the participants of the brainstorming session transfer the material from the flipchart onto small cards, one card for each problem/suggestion. Mix the pack of cards and divide it up in groups (6–8 persons in one group). Let the working groups discuss: why are we suffering from this problem? How can we solve it? Structure the material according to an analysis chart. It will help you to maintain an overview when there is a lot to be considered.

For a public service organizational development you might want to use the following analysis model (you can draw up a comparable chart for any field you are dealing with):

1. *External factors*
1.1 Legal regulations and directives.
1.2 The overall economic situation.
1.3 Politics and society.

2. *Organizational structure*
2.1 Definition of job assignment to various departments on the same level (horizontal structure).
2.2 Distribution of responsibility at different levels in the organization (delegation, vertical structure).
2.3 Flexibility in project work (interdisciplinary teamwork).

3. *Visions, goals and strategy*
3.1 Visions, goals and strategy.
3.2 Control routines, internal flow of information.
3.3 Information to/from external target groups.

4. *Culture, staff and working atmosphere*
4.1 Recruiting and induction of new staff.
4.2 Promotion.
4.3 Training.
4.4 Attitude to work, communication, motivation.
4.5 Culture, working atmosphere.

5. *Administration (technical equipment and working routines)*
5.1 Office accommodation and equipment.
5.2 Working routines.
5.3 Time management and personal planning.

6. *External relations to customers and clients*
6.1 Attitude to service.
6.2 Quality of service.
6.3 Availability.

During a brainstorming session between 200 and 300 suggestions might be made. In this case it is recommended to undertake a further sorting, whereby within a given category (5.1 or 3.2, etc), similar problems are gathered together in one problem group ('pattern'). For example:

2.1.1 *Imprecise definition of job-assignment*
    5    Overlapping job-assignment.
  102    Too much duplication.
   34    Grey areas.
  267    One hand does not know what the other hand is doing.

(The figure preceding the text indicates the problem number.)

This method allows you to reduce 200–300 suggestions to 20 or less. Now you really have an overview.

*Assessing suggestions*   Discuss the advantages and disadvantages of the suggestions with your staff. In this context I recommend the PMI-method (cf. exercise 12).

Some suggestions will certainly be too expensive, too time-consuming or untenable for other reasons. Remember: the waste-paper basket is man's best friend!

*Sorting out priorities*   You cannot do everything at once. Regular tasks should not be neglected just because everyone is involved in organizational development. You must sort out priorities.

You will find relevant methods in exercise 19.

*Plan of action*   Answer the following questions:

| | |
|---|---|
| What? | Be concrete. Avoid generalizations: tomorrow everything has to change completely. |
| Who? | Name names, and do not shelve solving the problem by imprecise formulations such as 'everybody'. |
| When? | Decide on a definite date: 'On 1 September', and not 'as soon as possible'. |
| How? | Propose ideas how the problem can be solved. |
| Where? | Agree on place, branch, department, etc. |

# Exercise 26 | Pin-pointing the problem

**Goals**

**177**  The aim of this exercise is to help you to find out: What is the problem and what is not the problem? This is important, because in a conflict people often focus on the wrong issue. This might be due to poor communication (they don't express themselves clearly), or lack of mutual trust (they are afraid of revenge, and don't dare to tell each other how they really feel). As a result you waste both time and energy on unproductive quarrelling. Therefore, it is worth trying to penetrate to the heart of the matter. By defining the problem precisely you have already taken a great step along the road to solving it.

**Possible snags**

Be aware that people often rationalize their feelings. They say 'He has broken the rules' when they mean 'I feel hurt'. Therefore, create a relaxed atmosphere, take enough time to carry out a thorough analysis, and do not be satisfied until people open up and say what they are really worried about.

To penetrate to the heart of the matter, invite those affected to a meeting where everybody has the opportunity to present their definition of what the problem really is. Write all suggestions on a flipchart, give room for discussion, and try to find the essence. For example:

In a small company some people worked overtime and others didn't. Under the surface the handling of overtime nurtured discontent. The good working atmosphere was in danger of being spoiled. By bringing the problem to the surface and undertaking a brainstorming session to define the problem, the following suggestions emerged:

- 'How should overtime be paid?'
- 'Why do some staff do overtime and others do not?'
- 'How can we work more effectively to avoid overtime?'
- 'How can we improve our project scheduling?'
- 'Is overtime exclusively negative?'
- 'Could we use ordinary working time more effectively?'
- 'Who should do overtime?'
- 'How can we anticipate and plan overtime better?'
- 'Why do we not have definite regulations governing overtime?'
- 'What motivates people to do overtime?'
- 'Would it be better to employ extra people rather than doing overtime?'
- 'Is overtime a temporary or a permanent problem?'

After a discussion it turned out that 'overtime' was not really the problem. What really mattered was that staff in one section were allowed to work overtime while others were not. This was regarded by the 'have-nots' as discrimination in respect to 'fringe benefits'. They also felt that the boss in the section allowing overtime cared more for his staff than the other section leaders. By pin-pointing the problem they found out that it was really equal treatment for everybody they were concerned about, and not overtime in itself.

## Exercise 27 | Saving money: administrative value analysis

**Goals**
With this method you can make savings of up to 20%. This is particularly true of companies which, over the years, have allowed their bureaucratic apparatus to become overweight.
**Possible snags**
The administrative value analysis is not suitable for companies which have already been thoroughly rationalized or suffer from a lack of qualified personnel.

Too little information about what is going to happen and why can result in negative attitudes on behalf of those affected by the savings measures.

**A word to the manager**

Your company has to reduce its costs. Instead of the management deciding everything themselves – a sure method of angering the entire staff – you can draw the staff into the process. After all, each person knows their field of work best. If those involved participate actively, the quality of suggestions is better.

**Rules for the administrative value analysis**

Call in a meeting and inform the staff on the why, the what and the how. Choose an internal project group or an external consultant to facilitate the process.

Step 1  *Achieving an overview*
Each individual member of staff notes down his specific tasks:

- What are the end products of my work in a month?
- Who are my clients (internally and externally)?

- How much time do I spend on each task?

Step 2   *Savings*
Imagine that as of tomorrow you will have 20–40% less resources (time, money, personnel) available to you:

- What would you do differently?
- Where could you make savings?
- What could you dispose of altogether?
- How could you work mor efficiently?
- What could you reduce in scope?

Step 3   *Evaluation*
The team evaluates the quality of suggestions by dividing them up into three categories:
- A   A terrific idea. Why didn't we think of it before? We'll definitely do it!
- B   We'll have to look into that more carefully. Is the result likely to justify the effort? Would the quality of goods and services suffer too much? Will our clients react negatively?
- C   No way! Straight into the waste-bin!

Step 4   *Analysis*
Thorough analysis of category B suggestions. They are either accepted (A) or rejected (C).

Step 5   *Plan of action*
Draw up a plan of action together:

- What?
- Who?
- When?
- How?

# Appendices

# Recommended reading

Adair, John: *Effective Teambuilding*. Gower Publishing Company, Aldershot, 1986.

de Bono, Edward: *Conflicts*. Harrap, London, 1985.

Dickson, Anne: *A Woman in Your Own Right – Assertiveness and You*. Quartet Books, London, 1982.

Evans, Roger and Russell, Peter: *The Creative Manager*. Unwin Paperbacks, London, 1989.

Fritz, Robert: *The Past of Least Resistance*. Ballantine Books, New York, 1984.

Gordon, Thomas: *Leader Effectiveness Training*. Peter Wyden, New York, 1977.

Hastings, Colin, Bixby, Peter and Chaudhry-Lawton, Rani: *The Superteam Solution: Successful Teamworking in Organisations*. Gower Publishing Company, Aldershot, 1986.

Jenks, M. James and Kelly, John M.: *Don't Do, Delegate*. Kogan Page, London, 1985.

Laborde, Genie Z.: *Influencing with Integrity*. Syntony Publishing, Palo Alto, 1984.

Leeds, Dorothy: *Smart Questions for Successful Managers*. Piatkus, London, 1988.

Loden, Marilyn: *Feminine Leadership or How to Succeed in Business Without Being One of the Boys*. Times Books, Random (UK), 1985.

McCormack, Mark H.: *What They Don't Teach you at Harvard Business School*. Fontana/Collins, London, 1984.

Moine D.J.: *Modern Persuasion Strategies*. Prentice-Hall, Hemel Hempstead, 1984.

Morrison, Ann M.: *Breaking the Glass Ceiling*. Addison-Wesley Publishing, Reading (Massachusetts), 1989.

Parker, Marjorie: *Creating Shared Vision*. Dialog International, Clarendon Hills (Illinois), 1991.

Rickards, Tudor: *Creativity at Work*. Gower Publishing Company, Aldershot, 1988.

Senge, Peter: *The Fifth Discipline*. Doubleday, New York, 1989.

Sher, Barbara and Gottlieb, Annie: *Teamworks!* Warner Books, New York, 1989.

Smith, Manuel: *When I Say No, I Feel Guilty*. Bantam Books, London, 1981.

Spencer S. and Adams J.D.: *Life Changes*. Impact Publishers, San Luis Obispo (California), 1990.

Tannen, Deborah: *You Just Don't Understand; Women and Men in Conversation*. Ballantine Books, New York, 1990.

# Model questionnaire for identifying motivating factors

The objective of this survey is to discover what motivates the staff in your company and what de-motivates them. Precise knowledge on these points is the precondition for a tailor-made project in management training and staff development.

**A word to the manager**

It is essential that the questions are answered anonymously. Therefore, it is recommended that the completed forms should be sent directly to an external consultant. If you use an internal consultant make sure that he/she really uses discretion. The person in charge of the survey must make sure that it is impossible to find out who has answered what. The respondents must have access to the final result.

**A word to the respondents**

This is your chance to contribute to a better working atmosphere. Answer the following questions spontaneously, and only discuss them with your colleagues after you have returned your question-naire. What is important is to capture the thoughts and feelings of the individual, and not the result of a group discussion on what staff are *supposed* to think and feel. Good luck!

**1 Your job**

*1.1* (a) How important is it to you to be able to increase your specialized knowledge within the framework of your job?

| −2 | −1 | 0 | +1 | +2 |

I am particularly interested in training further in the following fields:

(b) How important is it to you to have opportunities for developing your personality within the framework of your job (e.g. training in communicating with others, solving conflicts, relaxation techniques, self-management, etc)?

| −2 | −1 | 0 | +1 | +2 |

I am particularly interested in training further in the following fields:

1.2 (a) What opportunities does the company offer for training in your special field?

| −2 | −1 | 0 | +1 | +2 |

(b) What opportunities does the company offer for human development?

| −2 | −1 | 0 | +1 | +2 |

1.3 How would you rate your feeling of personal well-being at work?

| −2 | −1 | 0 | +1 | +2 |

**2 Objective and strategy**

2.1 Describe, in your own words, what you consider to be the company's principal objective.

2.2 Describe, in your own words, what you consider to be the management's strategy in striving to achieve this objective.

### 3 Attitudes to reorganization

3.1   The staff of a company are frequently sceptical about the necessity for re-organization.

    (a)   Have you observed negative attitudes of this kind in the company?

        Yes          no          don't know

    (b)   If the answer is yes:

        Which?

        What do you think are the reasons?

3.2   What do you think the management or your immediate boss can do to motivate the staff to regard change as a challenge rather than a threat?

3.3   What can you yourself do?

### 4 Working in project groups

4.1   Does project-group work function in your opinion?

    $-2$        $-1$        $0$        $+1$        $+2$

4.2   Have you any suggestions for improvement? What are they?

4.3   Does your group leader/boss listen to your opinion?

    $-2$        $-1$        $0$        $+1$        $+2$

4.4   How do you rate your chances of participating actively in what is going on?

    $-2$        $-1$        $0$        $+1$        $+2$

4.5   How do you rate the flow of information within the company?

        – too little information
        – too much superfluous information
        – it is totally unpredictable who will get what information
        – it is difficult to contact the responsible person

**187**

– information is made available at the wrong time
    (a) too early
    (b) too late
– are there other problems related to the flow of information? what?

4.6 | What do you consider to be the quality of departmental (specialized fields) meetings?

- very good
- good
- not very good
- badly prepared
- badly chaired
    (a)   too authoritarian
    (b)   poorly structured
    (c)   too unwieldy
    (d)   other problems?
- too many meetings
- too few meetings
- meetings too long
- meetings too short

4.7 | The working methods and techniques are:

- efficient
- not very efficient
- motivating
- boring
- depend on the personality of the person chairing the meeting
- haphazard
- precisely geared to the type of project
- other remarks?

**5 Relations between superiors and staff**

5.1 | Is your immediate superior a good listener?

  −2        −1        0        +1        +2

5.2 | Does your immediate superior give reasons for not following your advice?

|  −2        −1        0        +1        +2

| 5.3 | As a member of staff, are you involved in the decision-making process? |

-2          -1          0          +1          +2

| 5.4 | Are individual members of staff treated differently? |

Yes          no          don't know

If the answer is yes:

- Some are the boss's pets, others are ignored.
- At our place it is an advantage to be a woman.
- At our place it is an advantage to be a man.
- Other remarks?

| 5.5 | How do you rate the quality of staff meetings? |
(a)  Form of the meeting

-2          -1          0          +1          +2

(b)  Realization of plans

-2          -1          0          +1          +2

(c)  What do you personally expect from a staff meeting?

(d)  Do you have any concrete suggestions for improvement? What?

| 5.6 | Do you think the demands made on you correspond to your actual potential? |

- yes.
- unclear demands. I often do not know what is expected of me.
- too many demands. I already have more than enough to do and cannot face greater pressure of work.
- too few demands. My work hardly gives me a chance to realize my potential.
- sometimes yes, sometimes no. I cannot recognize any definite strategy on the part of my superior.
- other remarks?

**189**

## 6 Communication

6.1    To what extent do you think employees feel secure enough to say what they really think about something, even when it concerns a controversial matter?

     −2        −1        0        +1        +2

6.2    How important is praise and recognition to you?

     −2        −1        0        +1        +2

6.3    Do you get the positive feedback you deserve and expect on a daily basis?

     −2        −1        0        +1        +2

6.4    How important is it to you to receive constructive criticism from which you can learn something?

     −2        −1        0        +1        +2

6.5    Do you get constructive criticism on a daily basis when you have made a mistake?

     −2        −1        0        +1        +2

6.6    Does your immediate superior take enough notice of your work?

     −2        −1        0        +1        +2

6.7    Do you think you receive too much unspecific and exaggerated (negative) criticism when you have made a mistake?

     −2        −1        0        +1        +2

6.8    How do you rate the working atmosphere?

     −2        −1        0        +1        +2

6.9    Is there much office politics and unkind gossip?

   Yes        no        don't know

**7 Motivation**

7.1 | What motivates you?

7.2 | What de-motivates you?

7.3 | What can your immediate superior do to help you enjoy your work more?

7.4 | What can you yourself do to help you enjoy your work more?

**8 Management and staff development**

8.1 | How do you rate in-house measures relating to:

(a) Management training:

$$-2 \qquad -1 \qquad 0 \qquad +1 \qquad +2$$

(b) Human development:

$$-2 \qquad -1 \qquad 0 \qquad +1 \qquad +2$$

8.2 | Do you think it would be desirable for managers and their staff to participate in the same training measures?

$$-2 \qquad -1 \qquad 0 \qquad +1 \qquad +2$$

8.3 | Have you any suggestions for improving management and staff development? Please specify them.

# Index

# Project Leadership

## Wendy Briner, Michael Geddes and Colin Hastings

The world of project management is changing fast. There is less concern with planning and control and more with the management of people. There is a growing tendency to use projects as a mechanism for creating change. The net result has been the emergence of a new role, that of project leader.

Over a number of years the authors of this book have worked with the new breed of project leaders, both as consultants and on their unique training course "Leading Projects Efficiently". They have also studied the many ways in which projects are being used in activities as diverse as manufacturing, financial services, retailing, entertainment and politics.

Their book has little to say about the traditional techniques of planning and control, since the new style of project leader finds them inappropriate or limited. Instead it concentrates on the personal skills required, including an awareness of the organizational context and the political dimensions. The book ends with a powerful, provocative "action summary" and a guide to further sources of development.

## Contents

1993       192 pages       0 566 07421 4

# A Gower Paperback

# Right Every Time
## Using the Deming Approach

Frank Price

Over the five years since the publication of Frank Price's book *Right First Time* the business landscape of the Western World has undergone an upheaval - a Quality Revolution. This explosion of interest in the management of quality has not just affected the manufacturing sector but has influenced all areas of industry; and with diverse effects. In *Right Every Time* the author not only examines the content of quality thinking, the statistical tools and their application to business processes; he also explores the context, the cultural climate, in which these tools are put to work, the environment in which they either succeed or fail. The core of the book consists of a critique of Deming's points - which the author refers to as the new religion of quality - and an examination of the pitfalls which act as constraints on quality achievement. This is more than a 'how to' book, it is as much concerned with 'how to understand what you are doing', and the book's message is applicable to anybody engaged in providing goods or services into markets where 'quality' is vital to business success. There can be no doubt concerning the benefits of quality control, and in this important and highly readable text Frank Price reveals how such visions of excellence may be transformed into manufacturing realities.

## Contents

The Long-Neglected Tools of Quality • Deming's First Point • Deming's Second Point • Deming's Third Point • Deming's Fourth Point • Deming's Fifth Point • Deming's Sixth and Thirteenth Points • Deming's Seventh, Tenth and Eleventh Points • Deming's Eighth, Ninth, Twelfth and Fourteenth Points • Who Needs Religion? • Select bibliography • Index.

1993     192 pages     0 566 07419 2

# A Gower Paperback

# Problem Solving in Groups
## Second Edition

### Mike Robson

Modern scientific research has demonstrated that groups are likely to solve problems more effectively than individuals. As most of us knew already, two heads (or more) are better than one. In organizations it makes sense to harness the power of the group both to deal with problems already identified and to generate ideas for enhancing effectiveness by reducing costs, increasing productivity and the like.

In this revised and updated edition of his successful book, Mike Robson first introduces the concepts and methods involved. Then, after setting out the advantages of the group approach, he examines in detail each of the eight key problem solving techniques. The final part of the book explains how to present proposed solutions, how to evaluate results and how to ensure that the group process runs smoothly.

With its practical tone, its down-to-earth style and lively visuals, this is a book that will appeal strongly to managers and trainers looking for ways of improving their organization's and their department's performance.

### Contents

Part I: Introduction • The benefits of group problem solving • Problem-solving groups • Part II: Problem-Solving Techniques • The problem-solving process • Brainstorming • Defining problems clearly • Analysing problems • Collecting data • Interpreting data • Finding solutions • Cost-benefit analysis • Part III: Following Through • Presenting solutions • Working together • Dealing with problems in the group • Index.

1993     176 pages     0 566 07415 X

# A Gower Paperback

# How to Write Effective Reports

## Second Edition

John Sussams

In business, administration and research, the report is an indispensable tool and all managers or specialists need to master the skills involved in writing one. John Sussams' book covers all aspects of the subject in a thoroughly practical fashion. It not only discusses language and style but also explains how to structure and organize material to facilitate understanding. In addition it deals with planning, presentation and production.

The text is enlivened by examples and illustrations and there are a number of exercises designed to improve the reader's report-writing ability. This new edition reflects recent developments and includes a section on the latest word-processing and desktop publishing techniques.

## Contents

Why a Report?: Working papers; Other means of communication • Structure: The summary; The main body of the report; Complex ideas; Appendices; Charts and diagrams; Presentation of statistical data • Layout: Margins; Paragraphs; Headings; Numbering of diagrams, tables, and appendices; Spacing; When to print on both sides of the paper; Summary • Language • Spelling and Punctuation: Spelling; Punctuation; Italics; Numbers; Abbreviations • Materials and Equipment: Covers; Binding; Paper; Typefaces; Reprographic methods; Charts and diagrams • Planning: The schedule; The skeleton report; Assembling the raw material; Drafting; Timing; Editorial control • Exercises • Suggested further reading.

1993      144 pages      0 566 07476 1

# A Gower Paperback

# The Green Guide to Profitable Management

Kit Sadgrove

A survey of companies conducted by the author on behalf of David Bellamy Associates showed that:

- 94% of companies thought that environmental pressures would increase
- 75% believed they conformed to legislation, but most had not taken any steps to check their legal position
- Only 3% had commissioned an independent environmental audit

The question for today's companies is no longer *whether* to 'go green', but *how* to implement green policies which also make sound commercial sense. Reducing waste, for instance, benefits both business and environment. Sadgrove cites numerous examples - such as the company that invested in a system which cut out water pollution, and saved itself £75,000 a year. *The Green Guide to Profitable Management* offers practical solutions for individuals across the business and public sector. Real life case histories, specimen policies, charts, diagrams, and over 60 checklists show how you could begin to implement a greener approach tomorrow.

## Contents

List of checklists • List of illustrations • Foreword •Preface • Acknowledgements • Going Green • The Environmental Audit • Land and Buildings • The Office • Buying • Production • Engineering • Transport • Research and Development • Marketing • Public Relations •Personnel • The Cafeteria • Medical • Finance • Putting It All Together: The Environmental Management System • Appendix I UK Environmental Law • Appendix II Prescribed Processes and Substances • Appendix III Hazardous Substances • Appendix IV Glossary • Appendix V Useful Addresses • Index.

1994     276 pages     0 566 07542 3

# A Gower Paperback

# Gower Handbook of Management Skills
## Second Edition

### Edited by Dorothy M Stewart

Today's competitive business world demands managers with all round skills, from time management to teambuilding. For many managers, simply finding the time for skills training can be a major problem.

This second edition of a bestselling Gower handbook brings together the expertise of its specialists. Between them they cover the whole range of personal skills needed by today's managers. Checklists of key points for each chapter and a thorough index allows busy managers to easily locate guidance on specific areas.

- Part 1: Personal skills – from effective speaking to managing stress, and from time management to career planning
- Part 2: People skills – from recruitment to teambuilding
- Part 3: Practical skills needed for running departments: production, personnel, marketing and finance
- Part 4: Managing the business: strategic planning, accounting, negotiating and problem solving.

1994     563 pages     0 566 07614 4

# A Gower Paperback

# Gower Handbook of Management
## Third Edition
### Edited by Dennis Lock

*The Gower Handbook of Management* first appeared in 1983. It was acclaimed by reviewers and quickly established itself as a standard work. It covers the entire spectrum of management activity: strategy, operations and personal skills.

This third edition follows the pattern on which the success of the earlier editions was based. Its objectives and structure remain the same but the scope has been extended considerably. The text has been thoroughly revised and ten completely new chapters have been added, including chapters on quality and culture. Every chapter now ends with details of further reading for those who wish to pursue any subject in greater depth.

The handbook now contains seventy three chapters, each contributed by an authority on the subject in question. It remains the most comprehensive single-volume guide to management practice in the English language.

Summary of Contents
Part 1: Principles, policy and organization • Part 2: Financial management • Part 3: Marketing and sales management • Part 4: Research, development and design • Part 5: Purchasing and inventory management • Part 6: Production and project management • Part 7: Logistics management • Part 8: Administration • Part 9: Human resource management • Part 10: The skills of management • Index.

1993     1044 pages     0 566 07477 X

# A Gower Paperback

# The Goal

## Beating the Competition

## Second Edition

Eliyahu M Goldratt and Jeff Cox

Written in a fast-paced thriller style, *The Goal* is the gripping novel which is transforming management thinking throughout the Western world.

Alex Rogo is a harried plant manager working ever more desperately to try to improve performance. His factory is rapidly heading for disaster. So is his marriage. He has ninety days to save his plant - or it will be closed by corporate HQ, with hundreds of job losses. It takes a chance meeting with a colleague from student days - Jonah - to help him break out of conventional ways of thinking to see what needs to be done.

The story of Alex's fight to save his plant is more than compulsive reading. It contains a serious message for all managers in industry and explains the ideas which underlie the Theory of Constraints (TOC) developed by Eli Goldratt - the author described by Fortune as 'a guru to industry' and by Businessweek as a 'genius'.

As a result of the phenomenal and continuing success of *The Goal*, there has been growing demand for a follow-up. Eliyahu Goldratt has now written ten further chapters which continues the story of Alex Rogo as he makes the transition from Plant Manager to Divisional Manager. Having achieved the turnround of his plant, Alex now attempts to apply all that Jonah has taught him, not to crisis management, but to ongoing improvement.

These new chapters reinforce the thinking process utilised in the first edition of *The Goal* and apply them to a wider management context with the aim of stimulating readers into using the technique in their own environment.

1993     352 pages     0 566 07418 4

# A Gower Paperback

# A Systematic Approach to
# Getting Results

## Surya Lovejoy

'*Getting Results* is a practical handbook for making things happen', explains Surya Lovejoy. 'Today's managers are offered training in everything from understanding management accounts to power dressing, yet they are often left on their own when it comes to setting and meeting management objectives.'

Every manager has to produce results. This book is designed to equip managers with effective project management tools without drowning them in jargon. And whether the project is a conference, a sales target, or an office re-location, the principles are the same. You need a systematic approach for working out:

- exactly what has to happen
- when everything has to happen
- how to ensure that it does
- what could go wrong – and the implications
- how you will remain sane during the process

### Contents

Introduction • Turning a task into a project • Turning a project into an action plan • Creating and managing the budget • Creating project maps • Creating a winning team • Turning the action plan into action • Outwitting the paperwork • Remaining sane • Avoiding the technology trap • Crisis projects • Help! • After the project • Index.

1994     192 pages     0 566 07541 5

# A Gower Paperback

# The David Solution
## How to Liberate your Organization through Empowerment

### Valerie Stewart

As Jean Jacques Rousseau neglected to say: 'Organizations were created free, but everywhere they are in chains.' Whether you work in the private or public sector, in service, retailing, manufacturing or utilities, Valerie Stewart's new book will help you to demolish the blockages that prevent people in your organization from consistently delivering peak performance.

Written in a direct and entertaining style and enlivened with anecdotes, parables and case studies, it will show you: how to bust the bureaucracy; how to avoid paralysis by analysis; how to break down the barriers of organizational empire; how to empower junior managers; how to put customers first (yes, truly); and how to create an enabling culture.

### Contents
Chipping away the marble • Starting • Busting the bureaucracy • Paralysis by analysis • Cracking the corporate concrete • Empires, empowerment and entrepreneurs • Interlude • Customers first • The enabling organization • Teamwork for real • Transformational leadership • Values and principle • Appendix How organizations grow and change • Sources of further reading • Index.

1993      176 pages      0 566 07420 6

## A Gower Paperback

# Counselling Skills

## Robert de Board

All managers sometimes find themselves in counselling situations from time to time, usually without any training in how to handle the problem effectively.

This brief, down-to-earth guide examines some of the problems people at work are likely to encounter and describes one way of handling them that has been found highly successful. In a straightforward language, and using examples drawn from business life, the author shows what counselling involves in practice and explains some of its underlying ideas. He points out the considerable advantage of the method – and some of the pitfalls.

## Contents

Styles of helping • Predicting people's problems • The elements of counselling • Counselling and performance appraisal • Improving transactions • Journey into life-space • Developing the organization • Anxiety and stress at work • A checklist for counsellors • Appendices: Training for counselling • Further reading • Index.

1987      152 pages      0 7045 0563 0

# A Gower Paperback

# Assertiveness for Managers

## Terry Gillen

Do you, asks Terry Gillen, want to be the kind of manager who:

- motivates his or her team to achieve their objectives?
- inspires loyalty in subordinates?
- has the respect of colleagues?
- is highly regarded by senior management?
- feels self-confident at work?

Today's business environment is changing dramatically – and so is our understanding of management effectiveness, especially when dealing with people. A major requirement of successful managers is personal credibility; it helps them motivate staff, work better with colleagues and impress their 'superiors'. Personal credibility depends on the way managers interact with other – where they do so assertively they naturally exhibit the characteristics we value in other people and which staff admire particularly in a manager.

Terry Gillen's practical book opens with an assertiveness profile to help you assess your own skills. In Part One the foundations of assertiveness theory are related to the workplace. Workout pages assist skill development.

Part Two is a ready reference of how to behave assertively in a range of typical managerial situations.

1994     257 pages     0 566 07613 6

# A Gower Paperback